# POEMS

OF

# ALICE AND PHŒBE CAREY.

"IN THEIR DELICIOUS CLIME
MOCKING THE BIRDS WITH MORE MELODIOUS SONGS."

PHILADELPHIA:
MOSS AND BROTHER,
NO. 12 SOUTH FOURTH STREET.
1850.

*Stereotyped by L. Johnson & Co.*
*Philadelphia.*
*Printed by T. K. & P. G. Collins.*

# Advertisement.

---

The publishers but comply with the general desire, in issuing this first edition of the collected writings of the "two sisters of the West," Alice and Phœbe Carey, whose occasional contributions to the literary journals have within a few years secured for them a rank among the most popular writers of their sex in this country. It is believed that these leaves, gathered into a volume, will more than confirm the favourable judgments awarded to them upon their original and separate appearance.

*Philadelphia, Oct.* 1849.

# Notice of the Authors.

FROM GRISWOLD'S FEMALE POETS OF AMERICA.

AMONG the younger American poets there are few whom we regard with more interest, or whose writings inspire us with more hopeful anticipations, than these two sisters, who were born in a quiet and pleasant district in the vicinity of Cincinnati, where they have always resided. Their education has been limited by the meagre and infrequent advantages of an obscure country school, from which they were removed altogether at a very early age; and with neither books nor literary friends to guide or encourage them, and in circumstances which would have chilled and withered common natures, they "have been and still are, humble" but most acceptable "worshippers in the glorious temple of song."

ALICE and PHŒBE CAREY have but very recently become known at all in the literary world. It is but two or three years since I first saw the name of either of them, in a western newspaper, and of nearly a hundred of the poems which are now before me, probably not one has been written more than that time. "We write," observes Alice Carey, in a letter which I regret that I may not copy here entire, that the reader's affection might be kindled with his admiration, "we write with much facility, often producing two or three poems in a day, and never elaborate. We have printed, exclusive of our early productions, some three hundred and fifty, which those in your possession fairly represent." And these are the fruits of no literary leisure, but the mere pastimes of lives that are spent in prosaic duties, lightened and made grateful only by the presence of the muse.

In the west, song gushes and flows, like the springs and rivers, more imperially than elsewhere, as they will believe who study her journals, or who read these effusions and those of Amelia Welby, the authors of The Wife of Leon, and other young poets, whose minds seem to be elevated, by the glorious nature there, into the atmosphere where all thought takes a shape of beauty and harmony. A delicious play of fancy distinguishes much of the finest poetry of the sex; but Alice Carey evinces in many poems a genuine imagination and a creative energy that challenges peculiar praise. We have perhaps no other author, so young, in whom the poetical faculty is so largely developed. Her sister writes with vigour, and a hopeful and genial spirit, and there are many felicities of expression, particularly in her later pieces. She refers more than Alice to the common experience, and has perhaps a deeper sympathy with that philosophy and those movements of the day, which look for a nearer approach to equality, in culture, fortune, and social relations.

# Contents.

## POEMS BY ALICE CAREY.

## POEMS BY PHŒBE CAREY.

# POEMS BY ALICE CAREY.

---

## KEATS.

Till the future dares
Forget the past, his fate and fame shall be
An echo and a light into eternity.—SHELLEY.

ACROSS the southern hills comes the young May,
In her lap bearing, wet with honied showers,
White and blue violets, open to the day,
Blush roses, and the yellow cowslip flowers;
But from her o'er-full arms they lean away
Toward the melodious shadows of warm June,
Where their first love a pallid ghost doth stray,
Like a lorn maiden wailing 'neath the moon.

A very queen of beauty doth she move,
Waving her vermeil-blossomed wand in air;
While Hope with crimsoning cheek, and soft-eyed Love,
Sprinkle the yellow sunshine of her hair
With winking flower-stars, and the blue above
With its dropped hem of silver, beauteously
Edged with the sea-green fringes of the grove,
Tents her about with glory fair to see.

Alone I sit, and yet not all alone,
For unsubstantial beings near me tread;
At times I hear them piteously moan—
Haply a plaint for the o'er-gifted dead,
That, to the perfectness of stature grown,
Had filled the vacant heart of Time for aye
With a deep sea of melody unknown,
And sunken from the embracing light of day.

And yet alone, for not a human heart
Stirs with tumultuous throbbings the deep hush;
Almost the blue air seems to fall apart
From the delirious warble of the thrush—
A wave of lovely sound untouched of art,
That floats above me like embodied joy:
O for such wasteless dowery, to impart
Delight so dainty and without alloy!

Deep in the shady cincture of the vale
I hear a long and melancholy cry,
As a lost spirit might in anguish wail,
Clinging to sin, yet longing for the sky:
And o'er the hill-tops, crowned with verdure pale,
A gnarled oak lifts above its fellow trees
Its gray head, palsy-stricken by the gale,
Defiant of the lapse of centuries.

A golden cloud above the sunken sun
Holds the first star of the night's solemn train,
Clasped from the world's profaneness, like a nun
Behind the shelter of the convent pane:

Did the delicious light of such a one
  Fleck his dark pathway with its shimmering fire,
Whose fingers, till life's little day was done,
  Clung like pale kisses to the charmèd lyre?

I've read, in some chance fragment of old song,
  A tale to muse of in this lovely light,
About a maiden fled from cruel wrong
  Into the chilly darkness of the night;
Upon whose milk-white bosom, cold and long,
  Beat the rough tempest; but a waiting arm
Was reaching toward her, and in hope grown strong,
  Fled she along the woods and through the storm.

But how had he or heart or hope to sing
  Of Madeline or Porphyro the brave,
While the dim fingers of pale suffering
  Were pressing down his eyelids to the grave?
How could he to the shrine of genius bring
  The constant spirit of a bended knee,
Ruffling the horrent blackness of Death's wing
  With the clear echoes of eternity?

Hark! was it but the wind that swept along,
  Shivering the hawthorn, pale with milky flowers?
The swan-like music of the dying song
  Seems swimming on the bosom of the hours.
If Fancy cheats me thus, she does no wrong—
  With mists of glory is my heart o'erblown,
And shapes of beauty round about me throng,
  When of that musèd rhyme I catch the tone.

O lost and radiant wanderer of the storm,
Beauty eternal shines along the wave,
That bore thee on like an o'ermastering arm
To the blind silence of the hungry grave;
Nor genial spring, nor summer sunshine warm,
Broken to flakes of gold by boughs of gloom,
Hath power to make life's frozen current warm,
And the dark house of dust to re-illume.

Tell me, ye sobbing winds, what sign ye made,
Making the year with dismal pity rife,
When the all-levelling and remorseless shade
Closed o'er the lovely summer of his life?
Did the sad hyacinths by the fountains fade,
And tear-drops touch the eyelids of the morn,
And Muses, empty-armed, the gods upbraid,
When that great sorrow to the world was born?

Did Death stoop softly, and with gentle tone
Sweetly dispose his pallid limbs to rest,
As down the shadowy way he went alone,
With Love's young music trembling in his breast?
Then sunk as fair a star as ever shone
Along the gray and melancholy air;
And from Parnassus' hoary front, o'ergrown
With plants immortal, moaned infirm Despair.

Weave close, ye woods, your blooming boughs to-night,
Shut from my sense the joyous insect choir,
And all the intense stars whose wannish light
Checkers the wavy grass like spots of fire:

Nature for my sad thought is all too bright,
And half I long for clouds to veil the sky,
And softly weep for the untimely blight
Of all of him I sing of that could die.

The yellow leaves that covered up his grave
Are hidden by the monumental stone;
Immortal amaranths o'er his slumber wave,
And fame's deep trumpet to the world has blown
The echoes of his lyre. In her mute cave,
Silence shall lock *my* little song away,
And the vain longing for the fount that gave
*His* name to glory, perish with the clay.

---

## HANNIBAL'S LAMENT FOR HIS BROTHER.

In the rich shadows of a gorgeous tent
Sat the famed chief of Carthage, as through bars
Of heavy gold the day's last beams were sent;
And Eve, in her tiara of bright stars
And garniture of purple, to her breast
Like a fond mother, took her child to rest.
The boding phantom of his bosom brings
The Alps before him, with their icy crags,
For victory, with her broad and starry wings,
Is settling brightly on the Roman flags;
And as the silent shadows round him close,
His voice finds way through barriers of woes:—

"My lost, my fallen brother! can it be
That the proud beauty of thy brow is dim,
Bright victor of fierce battles? Is the dust
That hides the commonest soldier, strewed o'er thee?
And must thy falchion ignominious rust?
Yet, he fell bravely, not unworthy him
Who was the offspring of a battle-star,
And cradled in the bloody arms of war!
And 'tis my joy that he was not of those
Who shrink from peril; with a stoic's pride
He bared his bosom to his country's foes,
And, rushing to the combat, fought and died!
Lost star of glory! in my childhood's time
Thou wert my sweetest counsellor and guide;
And in the freshness of my manhood's prime
I wooed thee to my bosom as a bride:
But thou, whose banner in the dust is veiled,
With thee the aim of my existence died;
And Fear, that never until now assailed,
Sits like a mocking demon by my side!

"For hungry wolves, the Spartan mothers tore
The babes from their warm bosoms, every day;
And if they smiled not, they at least forebore
To give vain sorrow an o'ermastering sway:
And have I more to sacrifice than they?
Yes, time, in part, their losses might restore,
But mine must be remediless for aye.

"I hear the constant singing of the streams,
Down in the vineyards, beautiful and wide,—

O thou embitterer of my goldenest dreams,
  I thought to conquer thee before I died!
Ye gods! must I be rifled of that joy,
And taunted like a beardless, love-sick boy!
Yet have I battled with Rome's chiefest men,
  And triumphed gloriously; her brazen gates
Had not availed her haughty spirit then,
  Had I led firmly onward,—but the Fates
Made me their sport and plaything, when one blow,
Dealt by the hand of her eternal foe,
Had crushed her power and placed her at my feet,—
Her mighty heart my pillow: this were sweet!

"Gaul's proudest chivalry I've met in fight,
  And trampled them as reeds upon the plain;
Slaughtered at bay, and hunted down in flight,
  They cried for quarter, but they cried in vain;
And the blue waters of the Rhone that night
Stood red and stagnant, choked with heaps of slain!'

Were there no spectral shadows gliding there,
  O baffled champion, for thy country's weal?
No semblances of "angels with bright hair
  Dabbled in blood," to fix the damning seal
To a close-hugged ambition? Better dwell
  The lowliest shepherd of Arcadia's bowers,
Than mount to where the insatiate fire of hell,
  Like to a serpent's tooth, the heart devours!

## THE WRECK.

VEILED were our topsails to the blast; our helm was lashed a-lee;
And fearlessly our vessel drove before a stormy sea,—
O, safely in our midst that night had lain an empire's crown;
For every mariner had said our vessel must go down!

Some shrieked aloud; some humbly knelt, who never knelt before;
And some, with outstretched arms, looked forth toward the viewless shore;
And rougher still the rough wind blew, and heavier roll'd the sea,
Till every heart was poured in prayer, God of the storm, to Thee.

At length, about the middle watch, an aged man, and gray,
Right in the solemn hush, stood up, and said he could not pray;
And while, above our gallant deck, the mountain-billows broke,
Each soul forgot the storm, while thus the trembling sinner spoke:—

"I've been a rover of the seas these four-and-forty years,
And, in their darkest hours, my eyes have been ashamed of tears;
But now I fain would give myself an offering to the deep,
If I could say the prayers you say, or weep as you can weep.

"The blackest clouds along the sky, through which the thunders roll,
Are calm as peace, when measured with the tempest in my soul:
Once, when my heart was innocent, and joyous as a bird's,
My mother taught me how to pray—I cannot say the words.

"'Tis well that mother died so soon, for oft, I know, she smiled,
And talked about the happiness that waited for her child;
And I have been long years of those whose troublings never cease,
Aside from Virtue's pleasant ways and all her paths of peace.

"My spirit grew the house of pride; I scorned our humble cot,
And deemed that, for my lowliness, the world had loved me not.
Once, when the night was dark, like this, the thunder's roll as deep,
There was a whisper in my heart that would not let me sleep.

"I knew 'twas Satan telling me, Thou shalt not surely die;
And yet I went, as goes the bird, down to the serpent's eye.
Hard by my father's cot there dwelt a harmless man, and old,
Whose house was filled with merchandise and shining heaps of gold.

"That night I sought his dwelling out, and with a stealthy tread,
Winding the gloomy passages, I stood beside his bed.
I said the night was dark with storm; but, by the lightning's beam—
(Oh, would to Heaven the arm upraised had withered in its gleam)—

"I saw him: I have been, since then, in lighted halls of mirth—
In deserts vast, and palaces, and caverns of the earth—
A thousand and a thousand times I've sailed across the deep,
And that old man has with me been, awake, and in my sleep.

"Almost my heart misgave me once, so wan he looked, and old;
But when I turned to flee away, I saw the cursed gold;
And so I slew him,—twice he stirred, and once he feebly cried,
As with a rough and heavy stone I smote him till he died.

"Then clutching, in my bloody hands the prize, I fled away;
But shapeless things had followed me, that I could never slay.
Three days in the thick woods I hid, afraid of every sound,
And o'er and o'er I washed my hands in every pool I found.

"My guilt upon the withered leaves seemed writ, as on a scroll,
And every wandering wind I met was questioning my soul:
I thought the dead man's gold so thrilled the marrow in my bones,
And, seeking out a lonesome cave, I hid it in the stones.

"But still there were accusing tongues in herb, and flower, and tree,
And so I left the haunts of men, and wandered on the sea"—
Just then our fated vessel struck upon a rocky shore,—
One shriek arose, and all again grew silent as before.

I floated, as by miracle, upon the off-torn deck,
And knew not any living soul was with me on the wreck;
But when the morn, with misty eyes, looked down upon the tide,
That old man, with his arms across, was sitting at my side.

## I WOULD TELL HIM THAT I LOVE HIM.

I WOULD tell him that I love him, but I know my tongue would fail,
For his heart is proud and haughty, and would scorn the simple tale;
Since my feet have never wandered from the home where I was born,
Save among the pleasant meadows and the fields of yellow corn.

No! my lips shall never speak it, for he knows I love him now!
He has seen the burning blushes on my cheek and on my brow;
He has heard my accent falter when he said that we must part,
And he must have read the writing that is written in my heart!

Unlearned am I in eloquence, save that of gentle words,
And I never harked to music that was sweeter than the birds'—
O! if his haughty mother knew I loved but half so well,
She would hate me with a bitterness that words could never tell!

I've left my gentle sister and her ever warm embrace
When I knew that young Sir Richard would be coming
from the chase;
For somehow oft it chances in our rambles that we meet,
And I think—shall I deny it?—that a stolen kiss is
sweet!

Last night I dreamed I stood with him before a man
of prayer,
With the garland of white blossoms, that he gave me,
in my hair;
And he called me by a dearer name than sister, or than
friend—
O! how I wish so sweet a dream had never had an end!

Not for his lordly castles and his acres of broad land
Do I love young Richard Percy; for with but his heart
and hand,
A cabin in the wilderness, a cavern by the sea,
Or a tent in the wide desert, would be home enough
for me.

## THE SPECTRE WOMAN.

ALONG the hollow chancel the winds of autumn sung,
And the heavy flitting of the bat was heard the aisles among;
The sky was full of stars that night, the moon was at the full,
And yet about the old gray church the light was something dull.

And in that solemn churchyard, where the mould was freshly thrown,
Wrapped in a thin, cold sheet, there sat a lovely maid alone:
The dark and tangled tresses half revealed her bosom's charms,
And a something that lay hidden, like a birdling in her arms.

By that pale, sad brow of beauty, and the locks that fall so low,
And by the burning blushes in that lovely cheek, I know
She hath listened to the tempter, she hath heard his whisper dread,
When the "Get behind me, Satan," hath been all too faintly said.

It was not the willows trailing, as the winds among
them stole,
That was heard there at the midnight, nor the digging
of the mole;
Nor yet the dry leaves dropping where the grass was
crushed and damp,
And the light that shone so spectral was not the firefly's
lamp.

The pale moon veiled her beauty in a lightly passing
cloud,
When a voice was heard thrice calling to that woman
in the shroud!
But whether fiend or angel were for her spirit come,
The lips that could have told it have long been sealed
and dumb.

But they say, who pass that churchyard at the dead
watch of the night,
That a woman in her grave-clothes, when the moon is
full and bright,
Is seen to bend down fondly, but without a mother's
pride,
Over something in her bosom that her tresses cannot
hide.

## THE PAST AND PRESENT.

Ye everlasting conjurors of ill,
Who fear the Samiel in the lightest breeze,
Go, moralize with Marius, if you will,
In the old cradle of the sciences!
Bid the sarcophagi unclose their lids—
Drag the colossal sphinxes forth to view—
Rouse up the builders of the pyramids,
And raise the labyrinthian shrines anew;
And see the haughty favourite of the fates—
The arbiter of myriad destinies:
Thebes, with her "feast of lights" and hundred gates,—
And Carthage, mother of sworn enmities,
Not mantled with the desolate weeds and dust
Of centuries, but as she sat apart,
Nursing her lions, ere the eagle thrust
His bloody talons deep into her heart;—
Then say, what was she in her palmiest times
That we should mourn for ever for the past?
In fame, a very Babylon—her crimes
The plague-spot of the nations to the last!

And Rome! the seven-hilled city: she that rose,
Girt with the majesty of peerless might,
From out the ashes of her fallen foes—
She in whose lap was poured, like streams of light,

The wealth of nations: was she not endowed
With that most perilous gift of beauty—pride?
And spite of all her glories blazoned loud,
Idolatrous, voluptuous, and allied
Closer to vice than virtue? Hark! the sounds
Of tramping thousands in her stony street!
And now the amphitheatre resounds
With acclamations for the engrossing feat!
Draw near, where men of wars and senates stood,
And see the *pastime*, whence they joyance drank,—
The Lybian lion lapping the warm blood
Oozed from the Dacian's bosom. On the bank
Of the sweet Danube, smiling children wait
To greet their sire, unconscious of his fate.
Oh draw the wildering veil a little back,
Ye blind idolaters of things that were;
Who, through the glory trailing in their track,
See but the whiteness of the sepulchre!

Then to the Present turning, ye will see
Even as one, the universal mind
Rousing, like genius from a reverie,
With the exalted aim to serve mankind:
Lo! as my song is closing, I can feel
The spirit of the Present in my heart;
And for the future, with a wiser zeal,
In life's great drama I would act my part:
That they may say, who see the curtain fall
And from the closing scene in silence go,
Haply as some light favour they recall,
Peace to her ashes,—she hath lessened wo!

## DEATH OF CLEOPATRA.

The stars of Egypt's haughty crown
  Were settled on the brow,
And many a purple wave swept down
  From royal dust below.
Girt with the realms that owned her power,
  Enthroned in regal pride,
With priceless kingdoms for a dower,
  Imperial beauty died.

The spoils of cities overthrown
  Her broad dominion lined;
With pearls her palaces were sown
  As blossoms by the wind.
Her merchant-ships on every sea
  The royal flag unrolled,
Laden with spices heavily
  And fragrant oil and gold.

And yet from all the proud array
  That gather round a throne,
The queen imperious turned away,
  Sickened, and died alone.
How died she? Through her chamber dim
  Did songs and victories roll?
And were there fervent prayer and hymn
  Said for the parting soul?

Not so: they brought her robes of state,
 And decked her for the tomb,
And, cumbered with the gorgeous weight,
 She proudly met her doom:
And o'er the hand of heavy clay
 That once had guided wars,
In all their mocking beauty lay
 The purple and the stars.

Earth lent her soul no power to stem
 Such stormy waves as were;
And the sweet star of Bethlehem
 Had risen not for her.
O Thou, who daily givest its beams,
 Be the dark sins forgiven
Of her whose wild and mystic dreams
 Were all she knew of Heaven.

---

## PALESTINE.

Bright inspiration! shadowing my heart
 Like a sweet dream of beauty—could I see
Tabor and Carmel ere I hence depart,
 And tread the quiet vales of Galilee,
And look from Hermon, with its dew and flowers,
Upon the broken walls and mossy towers
O'er which the Son of man in sadness wept,
The dearest promise of my life were kept.

Alas! the beauteous cities, crowned with flowers,
And robed with royalty! no more in thee,
Fretted with golden pinnacles and towers,
They sit in haughty beauty by the sea:
Shadows of rocks, precipitate and dark,
Rest still and heavy where they found a grave;
There glides no more the humble fisher's bark,
And the wild heron drinks not of the wave.

But still the silvery willows fringe the rills,
Judea's shepherd watches still his fold;
And round about Jerusalem the hills
Stand in their solemn grandeur as of old;
And Sharon's roses still as sweetly bloom
As when the apostles, in the days gone by,
Rolled back the shadows from the dreary tomb,
And brought to light life's immortality.

The East has laid down many a beauteous bride
In the dim silence of the sepulchre,
Whose names are shrined in story, but beside
Their lives no sign to tell they ever were.
The imperial fortresses of old renown—
Rome, Carthage, Thebes—alas! where are they now?
In the dim distance lost and crumbled down;
The glory that was of them, from her brow
Took of the wreath in centuries gone by,
And walked the Path of Shadows silently.

But, Palestine! what hopes are born of thee—
I cannot paint their beauty—hopes that rise,

Linking this perishing mortality
  To the bright, deathless glories of the skies!
There the sweet Babe of Bethlehem was born—
  Love's mission finished there in Calvary's gloom;
There blazed the glories of the rising morn,
  And Death lay gasping there at Jesus' tomb!

---

## NAPOLEON AT THE DEATH OF DUROC.

Thou who movest through the tent-lights
  Like a cloud among the stars,
With the flags about thee streaming
  Like the shadows of red Mars;

Art thou he who lately slumbered
  By the Nile with turbans red,
While the children of the desert
  Wailed about thee for their dead?

Yes, thou'rt he whose standards fluttered
  Where the Rhine's bright billows flow,
And where brave men left their footprints
  Red in Hohenlinden's snow!

He, upon whose shattered columns,
  Darkened by the artillery's frown,
At the awful Beresina,
  Victory's starry wings came down!

From the plains of Rio Seco
To Siberia's mountain heights,
Glory with thy name is blended,
Hero of a thousand fights!

Yet thou movest through the tent-lights
Like a cloud among the stars,
With the flags about thee floating
Like the shadows of red Mars.

One thy great soul loves is dying,
One of courage true and tried,
And the spirit faints, and triumph
Fails before affection's tide.

Hark! the bursts of lordly music
On the midnight rise and fall!
Wounded Eagle of the Legion,
Wilt thou answer to its call?

Yes, the Imperial Guard are flying
Toward the dark tent of the king!
Death hath taken home his captive,
Is the tidings which they bring!

Therefore moves he through the tent-lights
Like a cloud among the stars,
With the flags about him trailing
Like the shadows of red Mars!

## THE ORPHAN GIRL.

My heart shall rest where greenly flow
  The willows o'er the meadow—
The fever of this burning brow,
  Be cooled beneath their shadow.
When summer birds go singing by,
  And sweet rain wakes the blossom,
My weary hands shall folded lie
  Upon a peaceful bosom.

When, Nature, shall the night begin
  That morning ne'er displaces,
And I be calmly folded in
  Thy long and still embraces?
Dearer than to the Arab maid,
  When sands are hotly glowing,
The deep well and the tented shade,
  Were peace of thy bestowing.

My soul was once a house of light,
  Whose joy might not be spoken;
But Fancy wore a wing too bright,
  And now my heart is broken!
But where the violets darkly bloom,
  And greenly flows the willow—
Down on the pavement of the tomb,
  There waits a quiet pillow.

## THE HOMELESS.

As down on the wing of the raven,
Or drops on the upas-tree lie,
So darkness and blight are around me
To-night, I can scarcely tell why!
Alone in the populous city!
No hearth for *my* coming is warm,
And the stars, the sweet stars, are all hidden
On high in the cloud and the storm!

The memories of things that are saddest,
The phantoms unbidden that start
From the ashes of hopes that have perished,
Are with me to-night in my heart!
Alas! in this desolate sorrow,
The moments are heavy and long;
And the white-pinioned spirit of Fancy
Is weary, and hushes her song.

One word of the commonest kindness
Could make all around me seem bright,
As birds in the haunts of the summer,
Or lights in a village at night;
But, lacking that word, on my spirit
There settles the heaviest gloom,
And I sit with the midnight around me,
And long for the peace of the tomb.

## A NORLAND BALLAD.

THE train of the Norse-King
Still wind the descents,
Leading down where the waste-ridge
Is white with his tents;
The eve-star is climbing
Above where they lie,
Like hills at the harvest-time,
Pale with the rye.

Who comes through the red light
Of bivouac and torch,
With footsteps unslackened
By fasting or march?
Majestic in sorrow,
No white hand, I trow,
Can take from that forehead
Its pale seal of wo!

Past grooms that are merrily
Combing the steeds,
To the tent of the Norse-King
He hurriedly speeds;
A right noble chieftain,—
That gloved hand, I know,
Has swooped the ger-falcon
And bended the bow.

Outspeaks he the counsel
He comes to afford—
"As loves this engloved hand
The hilt of my sword;
As loves the pale martyr
The sacrament seal,
My heart loves my liege lord
And prays for his weal.

"I once wooed a maiden,
As fair to my sight
As the bride of the Norse-King
I plead for to-night;
As thou dost, I tarried,
Her fond faith to prove,
And the wall of the convent
Grew up 'twixt our love.

"Hold we to our marching
Three leagues from this ridge,
And we compass our rear-guard
With moat and with bridge:
Give one heart such shriving
As priest can afford,
And a sweet loving lady
The arms of her lord!

"O felt you sweet pity
For half I have borne,
The scourgings, the fastings,
The lip never shorn;

You fain would not linger
  For wassail's wild sway,
But, leaping to saddle,
  Would hold on the way."

Outspoke then the Norse-King,
  Half pity, half scorn,
"Go back to thy fasting
  And keep thee unshorn;
No tale of a woman
  Pause I to divine;"
And from the full goblet
  His lip kissed the wine.

Then fell sire and liegeman
  To feasting and song;
I ween to such maskers
  The night was not long:
And but one little trembler
  Stood pale in the arch,
When gave the king signal
  To take up the march.

If danger forewarn him,
  The omen he hides,
And mounting right gayly,
  He sings as he rides:
"Now, bird of the border,
  Look forth for thy chief;
By the bones of St. Peter,
  Thy watch shall be brief!"

"Stand forth, wretched augur,"
He cries in his wrath,
As his foam-covered charger
Has struck on the path
Leading down to his castle;
"Stand forth, here is moat
And drawbridge to charge back
The lie in thy throat!"

"Pause, son of the mighty,
My bode is not lost
Till the step of the master
The lintel has crossed;
And then if my counsel
Prove ghostly or vain"—
The king smiled in triumph
And flung down the rein.

Lo! passed is the threshold,
None answer his call;
Why starts he and trembles?
There's blood in the hall!
His step through the corridor
Hurriedly flies,
'Tis only an echo
That answers his cries.

One pale golden ringlet
That kissed the white cheek
Of the sweet Saxish lady
They find as they seek:

There was mounting of heralds
  In hot haste, I ween,
But the bride of the Norse-King
  Was never more seen.

---

## MORNA.

Alas! 'tis many a weary day
Since, on a pleasant eve of May,
I first beheld her; slight and fair,
With simple violets in her hair,
And a pale brow of thought beneath,
That never wore a prouder wreath;
And roses hanging on her arm,
  Fresh gathered from the mountain side;
And wherefore, by her mien and form
  She is not mother, wife, nor bride?
Surely the hopes of childish years
  Still freshly on her girlhood rise;
But no, her cheek is wet with tears—
  What do they in those heavenly eyes?
The mournful truth they well belie;
  The roses, and the child-like form,
I know thee, by that look and sigh,
  A pale, sweet blossom of the storm.
And see! she pauses now, and stands
  Where step save hers has scarcely trod,

And softly, with her milk-white hands,
  Lays down her blossoms in the sod.
There is no marble slab to tell
  Who lies so peacefully asleep;
'Tis written on the heart as well,
  Of her who lingers there to weep.

One evening in the accustomed vale
  I missed the blossoms from the turf,
For Morna's lovely brow was pale,
  And cold as ocean's beaten surf.
That night I learned, beside her bier,
  The story of her grief in part.—
For much, that mortal might not hear,
  Lay hidden in her broken heart.
She was the child of poverty,
  And knew from birth its friendless ills;
But never blossom fair as she
  Grew up among her native hills.
Sweet child! she early learned to sigh;
  The roses on her cheek grew pale;
It matters not to tell the why—
  Who is there will not guess the tale?
He was the haughty child of pride—
  The angel of delusive dreams;
And therefore was she not a bride
  Who slumbers by her native streams.
The weeds of desolate years o'erspread
  The pathway where so oft she trod;
No mourner lingers o'er her bed,
  Or bears fresh blossoms to the sod.

## ALDA.

YOU would have loved her, had you seen;
The beauty of her life was prayer;
The sweet sky never wet with showers
A bed of yellow primrose flowers
As sunny as the lovely sheen
Of her loose hair.

O'er the low casement her soft hands
Twined tenderly the creeping vines;
Out in the woodland's shady glooms
Loved she to gather summer blooms,
And where, from yonder valley lands,
The river shines.

The rain was falling when she died,
The sky was dismal with its gloom,
And autumn's melancholy blight
Shook down the yellow leaves that night,
And mournfully the low winds sighed
About her tomb.

At midnight, near the gray old towers
That lift their lordly pride so high,
Was heard the dismal raven's croak,
From the red shadows of the oak,

And with her pale arms full of flowers,
The dead went by.

An old man now, with thin white hair,
Oft counts his beads beneath that tree;
Sometimes when noontide's glow is bright,
And sometimes in the lonesome night,
He breathes the dead girl's name in prayer
On bended knee.

A shepherd boy—so runs the tale—
Once, as he pent his harmless flocks,
Crossed the sweet maid, her lap all full
Of lilies pied, and cowslips dull,
Weaving up fillets, red and pale,
For her long locks.

Sweetly the eve-star lit the towers,
When, homeward riding from the chase,
Down from his coal-black steed there leapt
A courtier gay, whose dark plumes swept
A cloud of ringlets bound with flowers,
And love-lit face.

Summer is gone—the casement low,
With dead vines darkened—winds are loud;
Alda, no more the gray old towers
Shut from thee heaven's sweet border flowers.
Comb back the locks of golden glow,
And bring the shroud.

## THE PIRATE.

Elzimina! maid of ocean,
With the bosom of soft light,
Seest thou, settling down between us,
Stormy, never-ending night?
Through thy curtains of pale splendour,
As the rosy lamp-light falls,
Comes there not a memory, tender,
Of my dungeon's stony walls?

Elzimina! maid of ocean,
I can see thee, pale and meek,
Wiping with thy amber tresses
The salt waters from thy cheek—
Struggling like a beam of brightness
Towards my closing prison-door,
With thy arms of tender whiteness
Stretched to clasp me once, once more!

Elzimina! maid of ocean,
But the love of heaven's sweet shore
Or the dread of hell could tempt me
That dark parting to live o'er.
Will there not some mystic token
Fill thy heart with bitter pain
When the sod lies cold and broken
Where thy head so oft hath lain?

Elzimina! maid of ocean,
Rising from the hills I see,
Thin and white, the mists of morning,
That shall never set for me!
Wrecks of vessels lost and stranded
Filled thy soft heart with alarm,
And the gray wings, beating landward
Warned the sailor of the storm.

When, O lovely maid of ocean,
From the rocking deck with me,
Saw ye last the fiery sunset
Paint the arteries of the sea?
When the red moon's reddest shadow
Like a mantle clasped thy form,
And the green waves like a meadow
Rose and fell before the storm.

Elzimina! dream of beauty,
'Neath the lips that dare not speak,
Like the moonlight's falling crimson
Burned thy lily brow and cheek.
Destiny than will is stronger,
And thy gentle eyes must weep,
When my red flag lights no longer
The blue bosom of the deep!

Elzimina! maid of ocean,
Farewell now to thee and hope,
E'en thy white hands cannot save me
From the coiling gallows rope.

From the scaffold, newly risen,
  Creeps a shadow, dull and slow,
O'er the damp wall of my prison—
  God have mercy on thy wo!

---

## THE ORPHAN'S DREAM OF LOVE.

Oh! how my very heart could weep
  To think that none will see nor know;
Love's fountain may be still when deep,
  And silent, though it overflow.
But blossoms may unheeded grow,
  Whose leaves the sweetest balm enfold,
And streams be noiseless in their flow
  That wander over sands of gold.
O love! thou word that sums all bliss—
  Thou that no language ever told—
Best gift of brighter worlds to this,—
  They err, and oh! their hearts are cold,
Who hope to speak thee:—such would seem
  A thing too little worth to prize,
And mine is an ideal dream
  The world can never realize!
They find, whose spirits blend with mine,
  Thy best interpreter a sigh;
Bring their wreath offering to the shrine,
  And lay their hearts down silently.

5

There comes at times, on viewless wings,
And nestles in my heart, a bird—
Of Heaven, I think—for oh! it sings
The sweetest songs I ever heard.
When first it came, 'twas long ago,
For childhood's years were scarcely by,
Summer and evening time, I know,
For stars were floating in the sky.
With sunbeams on the hills at play,
And gathering moss and braiding flowers,
I had been out the long, long day
Till twilight came with dewy hours;
And threading carelessly along
The pathway, through the starlit glen,
I heard this sudden flow of song,
Which I had never heard till then.
I recked not of the time I stayed
Enraptured, so the melting lay
With sweetness filled the thickening shade;
But when at length I turned away
The stars had streaked with silver beams
The dusky mantle midnight wore,
And I was dreaming such sweet dreams
As I had never dreamed before!
I was an orphan—childhood's years
Had passed in heaviness of heart;
No second self had soothed my tears,
Or in my gladness bore a part.
But then—perchance the thought was weak,
Though vainly by the lips supprest,

For aught of which the heart can speak
  Is never long a secret guest—
I thought that there might yet be won
  What in the world is daily found,
"Something to love, to lean upon,
  To clasp affection's tendrils round."
O, if love's dreams be all so sweet
  As those which then to me were given,
Two kindred spirits, when they meet,
  Must surely taste the bliss of heaven!
It may be, why I scarcely know,
  But so to me it never seemed,
It may be fancy made it so,
  But as I wandered on, I dreamed
That every thing I looked upon
  Was full of loveliness and light;
The starry wreath that night had on
  Before had never shone so bright.
And with such blessings in his path,
  I marvelled man should ever sin—
Oh! earth a crowning radiance hath
  When all is light and peace within!
But since that vision of the glen
  Long weary years have o'er me flown,
And left me what they found me then,
  Within the wide, wide world alone.

## THE BLUE SCARF.

THE soldier of an elder clime—
His bosom seamed with scars—
Has oft beguiled my wanderings
With legends of the wars.
Once, as we slacked our bridle-reins
To gain a rising hill,
He told a tale of other times
That I remember still.

Sunset was slanting rosily,
And every cloud on high
Was like a floating pyramid
Of blossoms in the sky.
"There's something," said the aged sire,
"In every thing I see
That brings again the lights and shades
Of other days to me:

"For one, of all my brethren
The bravest in the fight,
Stood with me in the crimson haze
Of just so sweet a night.
We heard, against the shelving rocks,
The dashing of the seas,
And saw the summer sun go down
From just such hills as these.

"There never was a stronger arm
In any field of war,
Nor heart that beat more fearlessly
Beneath a knight's broad star.
For ever in the hottest fight
We saw his scarf of blue:
His eye repelled the curious—
His name we never knew.

"He never joined in revelry,
And never wept the slain,
And never either smiled or sighed
For any loss or gain:
For when the wings of victory
Were shining o'er our host,
I've seen him in his tent as sad
As if the day were lost.

"Once grappling with an enemy
Whose fingers, dropping blood,
Left on his flaunting scarf their print—
I slew him where he stood.
For this he seemed to love me more
Than aught of living breath,
And at the peril of his soul
Thrice rescued me from death.

"And when all hacked with gaping wounds
That left me many a scar,
The long and weary watch was his
Of the blue scarf and star.

And when sweet voices called me back
From warfare's stern array,
He girt my heavy armour on
And shared my homeward way.

"The old ancestral hills, at last,
That overhung the sea,
Were reached, and eve put on a smile
As if to welcome me.
Then said the knight, most mournfully,
'Our path is one no more;
Thine to yon ancient castle leads,
And mine is by the shore.'

"When at the morning hour I saw
The heavy shades of night
Break sullenly and roll away
Before the welcome light,
Without a hand upon his rein,
As there was wont to be,
His steed, with all his housings on,
Stood champing by the sea.

"And there, all wet and tangled, lay
The bright blue scarf he wore,
Among the sea-weed and the sand,
Washed out upon the shore.
O there were dark imaginings—
They may have been untrue—
For blent with that insignia
Was all we ever knew."

## THE STRANGER'S EPITAPH.

'Tis but a sad and simple line,
Portraying well the sleeper's doom;
I pray it never may be thine—
Stoop down and read it on her tomb.
She gave it me the night she died;
I never sought to know the rest,
Believing that her maiden pride
Was fain to lock it in her breast.

"*She perished of a broken heart,*"—
In truth a sad and simple line;
If this her story doth impart,
I pray it never may be mine!

The time I never shall forget,
When, with her dark eyes full of tears,
She told me that the seal was set
Upon the limit of her years:
And even ere she ceased to speak
What secretly before I knew,
The hectic deepening on her cheek
Attested that the words were true.
It was not that she feared to lie
On the cold pillow of the tomb;
But sometimes, though we scarce know why,
The heart is full, and tears will come.

Whatever griefs were hers to bear,
They surely had no taint of sin;
A temple outwardly so fair
Could only have been pure within:
And sometimes when the fountain stirred
Too palpably within her breast,
A sigh, a tear, a broken word,
Have left her secret more than guessed.
As from this vale we watched the stir
Of the light billows of the sea,
Both sadly musing—I of her,
And she of any thing but me—
She warbled something in a tone
As light and joyous as a bird's,
(It never sounded like her own
Unless the heart were in the words,)
Something of summer fruit and flowers,
Of waving meadows and ripe grain—
Of home and hearth, and wedded hours,
Then pausing suddenly—" 'Tis vain,
'Tis more than vain," she sadly said,
" To nurse these haunting visions now:
The nuptial and the bridal bed
Were never meant for me and thou.
O thou for whom I could have died,
I am as nothing unto thee!
Well, hast thou not another bride,
And wherefore should I care to be?"
Then placing her thin hand in mine,
Half sad, half playfully, she said,
" I fain would have this simple line
Upon my tomb when I am dead."

Another evening came—the breeze
  Was lightly sporting with the wave,
And wild-birds dropping in the trees,
  Whose shadows rested on her grave.

Three summer-times the grass had grown
  Unshaven on her lowly bed,
And autumn's yellow leaves been strown
  As often o'er the slumbering dead,
When on the evening of a day
  As beautiful as that she died,
A harper and a maiden gay,—
  Haply she may have been his bride,
Haply a sister, or a friend,
  I know not,—but her joyous laugh
She checked, and here I saw them bend
  To read the stranger's epitaph.
And both alike were young and fair,
  And both were happy, it may be,
And yet, though lightly touched of care,
  Some dark thread in the destiny
Of one must surely have had place—
  Leaning against this solemn yew,
And muffling from the light his face,
  He wept as man may scarcely do;
It seemed as if some thought of pain
  By the sad epitaph was stirred,
For oft he turned, then came again,
  And read it over word by word.
The twilight's rosy hours went by,
  And evening deepened into gloom;

The last stars trembled in the sky,
And still I saw them by the tomb.
And once since then in every year,
What time the reaper loves to see,
I note the selfsame minstrel here,
And marvel what his grief can be.
She perished of a broken heart—
We can but guess the harper's fate;
But surely thus to die apart
Were better than to meet *too late!*

---

## THE BETRAYAL.

Tell me, when the stars are flashing
In the northern skies so blue,
Or when morning's tender crimson
Sweetly burns among the dew,
Comes there no reproachful whisper
From the mornings and the eves,
When Hope's white buds to full beauty
Opened like the faint young leaves?

Ay, thou feel'st, despite thy silence—
That betrayal burns thy cheek;
Even to Love's forgiving bosom
There be thoughts thou canst not speak!

From the roses of that bridal,
 The dark price of nameless wo,
Thou mayst not unbind the curses
 Till thy last of suns is low!

Lost and broken is the music
 That with beauty filled the night,—
Melted from the frozen branches
 Are the frost-stars glistening bright,—
When a maid with trembling bosom
 Watched a ne'er returning steed,
Cleaving through the silver shadows,
 On and on, his shaft-like speed!

Faint against the ringing pavement,
 Fainter still the hoof-strokes beat;
Scarcely can she tell the shimmer
 Of the flint-sparks from the sleet.
Years are gone: the village hill-tops
 Redden with the sunset's glow;
With a lap all bright with blossoms
 Still the summers come and go.

With a cheek grown thinner, whiter,
 And the dark locks put away
From a brow of patient beauty,
 Dwells the maiden of my lay;
Dwells she where the peaceful shadow
 Of her native hills is thrown,
Binding up the wounds of others
 All the better for her own.

## ANNUARY.

A YEAR has gone down silently
 To the dark bosom of the past,
Since I beneath this very tree
 Sat hoping, fearing, dreaming last.
Its crimson glories, like a flame,
 Are trembling to the wind's light touch—
All just a year ago the same,
 And I—oh! I—am changed so much!

The beauty of a wildering dream
 Hung softly round declining day;
A star of all too sweet a beam
 In eve's flushed bosom trembling lay.
Changed in its aspect, yet the same,
 Still climbs that star from sunset's glow,
But its embraces of pale flame
 Clasp not the weary world from wo!

Another year shall I return,
 And cross this solemn chapel floor,
While round me memory's shrine-lamps burn,
 Or shall this pilgrimage be o'er?
One that I loved, grown faint with strife,
 When drooped and died the tenderer bloom,
Folded the white tent of young life
 For the pale army of the tomb.

The dry seeds dropping from their pods,
  The hawthorn apples bright as dawn,
And the pale mullein's starless rods,
  Were just as now, a year agone.
But changed is every thing to me,
  From the small flower to sunset's glow,
Since last I sat beneath this tree,
  A year, a little year ago.

I leaned against this broken bough,
  This faded turf my footstep pressed;
But glad hopes, that are not there now,
  Lay softly trembling in my breast:
Trembling, for through the golden haze,
  Rose, as the dead leaves drifted by,
As from the Vala of old days,
  The mournful voice of prophecy.

Give woman's heart one triumph hour,
  Even on the borders of the grave,
And thou hast given her strength and power
  The saddest ills of life to brave.
Crush that far hope down, thou dost bring
  To the poor bird the tempest's wrath,
Without the petrel's stormy wing
  To beat the darkness from its path.

Once knowing mortal hope and fear,
  Whate'er in heaven's sweet clime thou art,
Bend, pitying mother, softly near,
  And save, oh! save me from my heart!

Hush, hush, pale-handed Memory,
  My knee is trembling on the sod—
An heir of immortality,
  A child of the eternal God.

---

## THE CHILDREN.

Come, sit down, little children,
  Beneath these green old trees,
There's such a world of sweetness
  In the kisses of the breeze:
Now push away the tresses
  From your young and healthful brows,
And listen to the music
  Up above us in the boughs.

How pleasant is the stirring
  Where the leaves are thick and bright;
And the wings of birds are floating,
  Like the golden summer light.
The fragrance of the brier-rose
  Is sweet upon the air;
And the pinks and dark-leaved violets
  Are scattered everywhere.

The lilies hang their silver cups
  Close to the water's edge,
And the pebbles are veined deeply
  As the berries in the hedge.

But where yon winding pathway
  Along the hill is trod,
'Tis the mourner's heavy footstep
  That has worn away the sod.

The smooth white stones, like spectres,
  Are standing in the shade,
To mark the narrow chambers
  Where the old and young are laid.
There hides the deadly nightshade
  Where the tall and bent grass waves;
And willow's tresses, long and sad,
  Are trailed above the graves.

Not with the gentle falling
  Of the early summer rain;
Not with the pleasant rushing
  Of the sickle in the grain;
Nor when the crimson mantle
  Of the morn is o'er them spread,
Shall the pale hands be unfolded
  From the bosoms of the dead.

But there's a morn approaching
  When the sleepers shall arise,
And go up and be with angels
  In the ever-cloudless skies.
Oh, earth is very beautiful
  With sunshine and with flowers;
But there's a world, my little friends,
  Of purer hearts than ours.

## TO MARY.

Oh, will affection's tendrils twine
About that summer time for aye,
When midway 'twixt thy home and mine
The quiet village churchyard lay!
With stars beginning to ascend,
And homeward winglets on the air,
Dost thou remember, O my friend,
How often we have parted there?

That summer, like a sunlit sea,
Reflected neither cloud nor frown,
Yet in its bright wave noiselessly
Some ventures of the heart went down!
Blest be the one that still outrides
The silent but tumultuous strife
Of hopes and fears, like heaving tides,
That beat against the shore of life!

The flowers run wild that used to be
So softly tended by thy hand—
Colours of beauty struck at sea,
And drifted backward to the land!
Breathing of havens whence we sailed,
Visions of lovelight seen and fled,
Swift barks of gladness met and hailed,
Of beacon fires, and land ahead!

A tumult of sweet light and shade
  Is trembling softly in my heart,—
A hush upon my soul is laid—
  Our paths henceforth must lie apart!
In the dim chamber where I sit,
  Fears, hopes, and memories rise and blend,
Like pale mists with the sunshine lit—
  God's blessing on thee, my lost friend!

---

## THE LOVER'S VISION.

THE mist o'er the dark woods
  Hangs whiter than snow,
And the dead leaves keep surging
  And moaning below!
Who treads through their dim aisles?
  Now answer me fair!
'Tis not the bat's flabby wing
  Beating the air!

A sweet vision rises,
  Though dimly defined,
And a hand on my forehead
  Lies cold as the wind!
I clasp the white bosom,
  No heart beats beneath;
On the lips, pale and lovely,
  There trembles no breath.

The red moon was climbing
  The rough rocks behind,
And the dead leaves kept moaning,
  As now, in the wind;
The white stars were shining
  Through cloud-rifts above,
When first in these dim woods
  I told her my love.

Half fond, half reproachful,
  She gazed in my face,
And, shrinking from, suffered
  My fervid embrace:
And speaking not, lingered
  With love's bashful art,
Till the light of her dark eyes
  Burned down to my heart!

Like the leaf of a lily
  When Autumn breathes chill,
The tiny hand trembled
  That now is so still;
And I knew the sweet passion,
  Her lips only sighed,
In the hush of her chamber
  The night that she died!

O'er the shroud of the pale one
  I made me a vow
To kiss back the crimson
  Of life to her brow;

If she from the still grave
  Would come, as she hath,
And walk at the midnight
  This lone forest path.

The cloud-rifts are closing,
  The white stars are gone;
But the hushed step of darkness
  Treads solemnly on.
I call the dead maiden,
  But win no reply—
She has gone, and for ever,—
  O God! I could die.

---

## MELODY.

Where white in the jungles
  Lay bones of the dead,
All night the wild lioness
  Howled as she fed:
The wind hot and sultry,
  And scarcely awake,
Through the dust of the desert-sand
  Crept like a snake.

But a beacon gleamed redly
  The blue rocks along,

Where a golden-tressed maiden
  Sat singing her song:
With her passionate warble
  The white sea-mist stirred,
And a boat to the desert shore
  Flew like a bird.

The deep burning blushes
  That cover her brow,
In a lover's embraces
  Are all hidden now.
Wild rover of ocean,
  Proud scorner of storms,
Guard fondly the treasure
  Thus clasped in thine arms.

As the eyes of the pilgrim,
  Wherever he be,
Turn, down-trodden city
  Of beauty, to thee:
Turn thou, in life's pauses
  Of dimness and care,
To the sweet love of woman,
  That all things will dare!

## TO LUCY.

THE leaves are rustling mournfully,
  The yellow leaves and sere;
For Winter with his naked arms
  And chilling breath is here.
The rills that all the autumn-time
  Went singing to the sea,
Are waiting in their icy chains
  For Spring to set them free.
No bird is heard the livelong day
  Upon its mates to call,
And coldly and capriciously
  The slanting sunbeams fall.

There is a shadow on my heart
  I cannot fling aside;
Sweet sister of my soul! with thee
  Hope's brightest roses died.
I'm thinking of the pleasant hours
  That vanished long ago,
When summer was the goldenest,
  And all things caught its glow:
I'm thinking where the violets
  In fragrant beauty lay,
Of the buttercups and primroses
  That blossomed in our way.

I see the willow, and the spring
  O'ergrown with purple sedge;
The lilies and the scarlet pinks
  That grew along the hedge;
The meadow, where the elm-tree threw
  Its shadows dark and wide,
And sister-flowers in beauty grew
  And perished side by side:
O'er the accustomed vale and hill
  Now Winter's robe is spread;
The beetle and the moth are still,
  And all the flowers are dead.

I mourn for thee, sweet sister,
  When the wintry hours are here;
But when the days grow long and bright,
  And skies are blue and clear—
Oh, when the summer's banquet
  Among the flowers is spread,
My spirit is most sorrowful
  That thou art with the dead.
We laid thee in thy narrow bed
  When autumn winds were high—
Thy life had taught us how to live,
  And then we learned to die.

## AN EVENING TALE.

Come, thou of the drooping eyelid,
  And cheek that is meekly pale,
Give over thy pensive musing
  And list to a lonesome tale;
For hearts that are torn and bleeding,
  Or heavy as thine, and lone,
May find in another's sorrow
  Forgetfulness of their own.
So heap on the blazing fagots
  And trim the lamp anew,
And I'll tell you a mournful story—
  I would that it were not true!

The bright red clouds of the sunset
  On the tops of the mountains lay,
And many and goodly vessels
  Were anchored below in the bay;
We saw the walls of the city,
  And could hear its vexing din,
As our mules, with their nostrils smoking,
  Drew up at a wayside inn:
The hearth was ample and blazing,
  For the night was something chill,
But my heart, though I knew not wherefore,
  Sank down with a sense of ill.

That night I stood on the terrace
  O'erlooking a blossomy vale,
And the gray old walls of a convent
  That loomed in the moonlight pale—
Till the lamp of the sweet Madonna
  Grew faint as if burning low,
And the midnight bell in the turret
  Swung heavily to and fro—
When just as its last sweet music
  Came back from the echoing hill,
And the hymn of the ghostly friars
  In the fretted aisle grew still—

On a rude bench, hid among olives,
  I noted a maiden fair,
Alone, with the night wind playing
  In the locks of her raven hair.
Thrice came the sound of her sighing,
  And thrice were her red lips pressed
With wild and passionate fervour
  To the cross that hung on her breast:
But her bearing was not the bearing
  That to saintly soul belongs,
Albeit she chanted the fragments
  Of holy and beautiful songs.

'Twas the half hour after the midnight,
  And, so like that it might be now,
The full moon was meekly climbing
  Over the mountain's brow—

When the step of the singing maiden
  In the corridor lightly trod,
And I presently saw her kneeling
  In prayer to the mother of God!
On the leaves of her golden missal
  Darkly her loose locks lay,
And she cried, "Forgive me, sweet Virgin,
  And mother of Jesus, I pray!"

When the music was softly melting
  From the eloquent lips of morn,
Within the walls of the convent
  Those beautiful locks were shorn:
And wherefore the veil was taken
  Was never revealed by time,
But Charity sweetly hopeth
  For sorrow, and not for crime.

---

## SAILOR'S SONG.

HA! the bird has fled my arrow—
  Though the sunshine of its plumes,
Like the summer dew, is dropping
  On its native valley blooms:
In the shadow of its parting wing
  Shall I sit down and pine,
That it pours its song of beauty
  On another heart than mine?

From thy neck, my trusty charger,
I will strip away the rein,
But to crop the flowery prairie
May it never bend again!
With thy hoof of flinty silver,
And thy blue eye shining bright,
Through the red mists of the morning
Speed like a beam of light.

I'm sick of the dull landsmen—
'Tis time, my lads, that we
Were crowding on the canvas,
And standing out to sea!
Ever making from the headlands
Where the wrecker's beacons ride,
Red and deadly, like the shadow
Of the lion's brinded hide;

And hugging close the islands,
That are belted with the blue,
Where a thousand birds are singing
In the dells of light and dew;
Time unto our songs the billows
With their dimpled hands shall keep,
As we're ploughing the white furrows
In the bosom of the deep!

In watching the light flashing
Like live sparks from our prow,
With but the bitter kisses
Of the cold surf on my brow,

May my voyage at last be ended,
And my sleep be in the tide,
With the sea-waves clasped around me,
Like the white arms of a bride.

---

## THE OLD HOMESTEAD.

WHEN first the skies grow warm and bright
And fill with light the hours,
And, in her pale, faint robes, the Spring
Is calling up the flowers,—
When children, with unslippered feet,
Go forth with hearts of glee,
To the straight and even furrows
Where the yellow corn must be,—
What a beautiful embodiment
Of ease, devoid of pride,
Is the good old-fashioned homestead,
With doors still open wide!

But when the happiest time is come
That to the year belongs,
Of uplands bright with harvest gold,
And meadows full of songs,—
When fields of yet unripened corn
And daily garnering stores
Remind the thrifty husbandman
Of ampler threshing-floors,—

How pleasant, from the din and dust
Of the thoroughfare aloof,
Seems the old-fashioned homestead,
With steep and mossy roof!

When home the woodsman plots, with axe
Upon his shoulder swung,
And in the knotted apple-tree
Are scythe and sickle hung,—
When light the swallows twitter
'Neath the rafters of the shed,
And the table on the ivied porch
With decent care is spread,—
The hearts are lighter and freer
Than beat in the populous town,
In the old-fashioned homestead,
With gables sharp and brown!

When the flowers of Summer perish
In the cold and bitter rain,
And the little birds with weary wings
Have gone across the main,—
When curls the blue smoke upward
Toward the bluer sky,
And cold along the naked hills
And white the snow-drifts lie,—
In legends of love and glory
They forget the cloud and storm,
In the old-fashioned homestead,
With hearth-stone ample and warm!

## LIGHTS OF GENIUS.

UPHEAVING pillars, on whose tops
The white stars rest like capitals,
Whence every living spark that drops
Kindles and blazes as it falls!
And if the arch-fiend rise to pluck,
Or stoop to crush their beauty down,
A thousand other sparks are struck,
That Glory settles in her crown.
The huge ship, with its brassy share,
Ploughs the blue sea to speed their course,
And veins of iron cleave the air
To waft them from their burning source!
All, from the insect's tiny wings,
And the small drop of morning dew,
To the wide universe of things,
The light is shining, burning through.
Too deep for our poor thoughts to gauge
Lie their clear sources, bright as truth,
Whence flows upon the locks of age
The beauty of eternal youth.
Think, oh, my faltering brother! think,
If thou wilt try, if thou hast tried,
By all the lights thou hast, to sink
The shaft of an immortal tide!

## I KNOW THOU ART FREE.

I KNOW thou art free from earth's sordid control,
In the beautiful mansions above—
That sorrow can never be flung o'er the soul
That rests in the bosom of Love.
I know that the wing of thy spirit is furled
By the palm-shaded fountains of bliss,
That erst in its strife for the bright upper world
Was bruised and enfeebled in this.

For oft as I gaze on thy dwelling of light,
When the glory of stars is on high,
I hear in my visions, as glowingly bright,
The flutter of wings in the sky:
And in the sweet islands that slumber afar
From the tomb and the desert and sea,
With glory around thee that nothing can mar,
My soul hath revealings of thee.

But still like a captive confined from the day,
My heart doth in bitterness pine;
And sigh for release from its prison of clay,
And a blissful reunion with thine:
Save when I am come to the heavenly shrine
To pour supplication and prayer,
For then doth my spirit seem nearer to thine,
And lay down its mantle of care.

## A GOOD MAN.

A MAN he was, of thin and silver hairs,
  Whose pious hands and never-wearied feet
Kept from a sacred field the enemy's tares,
  And nursed to vigorous growth the precious wheat.

Though he had loved and kept the rule of right,
  After the strictest manner, from his youth,
Often his prayer went up for larger light,
  And deeper, holier reverence for truth.

Hard by the village church his mansion stood,
  Modest of bound, yet hospitably wide;
His highest eloquence was doing good,
  His simple meekness the rebuke of pride.

Oh! vainly cheerful glowed the evening fire,
  Amply in vain the housewife's board was spread,
That night when homeward came the toil-worn sire
  And told his children the good man was dead.

Within God's holy temple there was wo—
  Wo that the Book of Life might scarce assuage;
The tremulous voice was dumb, and the white flow
  Of reverend locks swept not the sacred page.

Oft had that man of God, while living, said,
  Wherefore, my children, do you vainly weep?
The friend you mourn so sadly is not dead,
  But only fallen in the Lord asleep!

For he had preached, with zeal that would not cease,
  Christ and the resurrection, not in vain;
For, like a benediction full of peace,
  Came the blest memory to the weeping train.

And they rose up with souls less sadly dim,
  Young men, and maidens, and the bowed with care,
Feeling that death had only been to him
  God's hour of answer to a life of prayer.

---

## HYMN OF THE TRUE MAN.

PEACE to the True Man's ashes! Weep for those
  Whose days in old delusions have grown dim;
Such lives as his are triumphs, and their close
  An immortality. Weep not for him.

As feathers wafted from the eagle's wings
  Lie bright among the rocks they cannot warm,
So lie the flowery lays that Genius brings,
  In the cold turf that wraps his honoured form.

A practical rebuker of vain strife,
  Bolder in deeds than words, from beardless youth
To the white hairs of age, he made his life
  A beautiful consecration to the Truth.

Virtue, neglected long, and trampled down,
  Grew stronger in the echo of his name;
And, shrinking self-condemned beneath his frown,
  The cheek of harlotry grew red with shame.

Serene with conscious peace, he strewed his way
  With sweet humanities, the growth of love;
Shaping to right his actions, day by day,
  Faithful to this world and to that above.

The ghosts of blind belief and hideous crime,
  Of spirit-broken loves, and hopes betrayed,
That flit among the broken walls of Time,
  Are by the True Man's exorcisms laid.

Blest is his life who to himself is true,
  And blest his death—for memory, when he dies,
Comes, with a lover's eloquence, to renew
  Our faith in manhood's upward tendencies.

Weep for the self-abased, and for the slave,
  And for God's children darkened with the smoke
Of the red altar—not for him whose grave
  Is greener than the misletoe of the oak.

## HYMN OF THE STUDENT OF NATURE.

"I have learned to lean on my own soul, and not to look elsewhere for the reeds that a wind can break."—BULWER.

I KNOW my humble lineage—that my way
Has led among life's valleys, and does still;
But destiny is as the potter's clay,
And we can make it glorious if we will!

Smiles settled on the lips of one who died
In the quick tortures of a fiery bed;
And they by less severe ordeals tried
May surely to an equal strength be wed.

True many that I deemed my friends are gone,
But, Nature, thou at least wilt still be kind;
For from thy naked bosom I have drawn
The sweetest draughts I ever hope to find.

Out in the tents of summer I have heard
Music that made me happy, not of art,
But the wild song of some sweet-throated bird,
That flowed, as all things best do, from the heart.

I will not chase the phantoms that are fled,
Nor like a lovesick dreamer pray to die,

Though I may have no shelter for my head
  But the blue curtain of God's equal sky.

But in some flowery nook, away from care,
  Fanning my heart down to a pulse more even,
I'll build me beautiful palaces of air
  For my soul's children, beings sweet as heaven.

And these shall be my friends, for friends like these
  Can trouble with no yearning to depart,
And the cold kisses of the mountain breeze
  Wake not the tale of Indus in the heart!

---

## LIFE'S ANGELS.

O STILL, and dumb, and silent Earth,
  Unlock thy dim and pulseless arms;
Wandering and weary from her birth,
  Thy child seeks refuge from life's storms!

Still from my heart a shadow lifts,
  And through my soul a lost voice thrills,
As the soft starlight's golden drifts
  Sweep nightly o'er the western hills.

Life has its angels, though unkept
  The lovelight which their beauty brings,
And though the blue heavens are not swept
  With the white radiance of their wings.

But a dark shadow—not the grave's—
   Has clasped the one I loved from me,
And winds have built their walls of wave
   Between us in the eternal sea.

I dare not drink the mantling cup,
   Nor light the shrine in Love's sweet name,
Lest from the dark be lifted up
   Pale hands to smother down the flame.

The music on the lip of morn,
   Wings glancing on the summer air,
Love's rose-crown—all things earthly born—
   Are links that bind me to despair.

Whene'er the fires of sunset's glow
   Stream bright across some silver cloud,
I think about the wavy flow
   Of long loose tresses o'er the shroud.

No more I tremble with sweet awe,
   For all life's shining waves grow dim,
When there one burning star I saw
   Quench its bright axle to the rim.

Borne down and weary with life's storms,
   O Earth, receive me to thy breast;
Unlock thy dim and pulseless arms,
   And cool this burning heart to rest.

## THE PILGRIM.

THE child of an Eternal Sire!
  Great waves of burning desert sand
And mountains with their tongues of fire
  Are but as dew-drops in his hand.

O'ershadowed by the gallows tree,
  And moaning like the hunted Jew,
Our guilt is like a mighty sea,
  With God's sweet mercy shining through!

How deep that mercy, and how wide!
  The child of lost and recreant years
Can in a Father's bosom hide
  His sins, his sorrows, and his tears!

Once, when the noontide's fervid rays,
  Like sickles in the dim grass lay,
Bent forward on his staff to gaze
  For the loved city far away,—

I crossed a pilgrim, and I knew,
  More by an instinct of the soul
Than by his white hairs, thin and few,
  That he might never reach the goal.

And when I saw him onward start,
  With fainter hope, and step more slow,
God knoweth that within my heart
  The measure could have gauged his wo!

For I have seen all sad above,
  And all below in bitterest strife,
When e'en the planet of my love
  Sat darkly in my house of life.

And sometimes, my poor bleeding feet
  Far from the cooling fountain wave,
I've thought no shadow half so sweet
  As that which darkened o'er the grave!

The temples, palaces, and towers
  Of the old time, I may not see,
Nor 'neath my reverent tread, thy flowers
  Bend meekly down, Gethsemane!

By Jordan's wave I may not stand,
  Nor climb the hills of Galilee,
Nor break with my poor sinful hand
  The crosier of apostasy!

Nor pitch my tent 'neath Salem's sky,
  As faith's impassioned fervour bids,
Nor hear the wild bird's startled cry
  From Egypt's awful pyramids.

I have not stood, and may not stand
  Where Hermon's dews the blossoms feed,

Nor where the flint-sparks light the sand
  Beneath the Arab lancer's steed.

Wo for the dark thread in my lot,
  That still hath kept my feet away
From pressing toward the hallowed spot
  Where Mary and the young child lay.

But oh! I thank the gracious Power,
  That I, in nature's ponderous tome,
Can find a splendour in the flower,
  A glory in the stars of home.

And haply o'er those planets bright,
  That in the blue vault nightly spring,
Are farther worlds of larger light,
  Each counted as a little thing

By Him, who day's wide splendour planned,
  And gave, to glorify the night,
Those visible jewels of his hand—
  Saying at first, Let there be light!

But with great systems for his care,
  Beyond the farthest star we see,
He bends to hear the pleading prayer
  Of every sinful child like me.

And in the ashes of the fears
  That darken o'er the closing strife,
Faith, with her soft eyes full of tears,
  Strews blossoms from the Tree of Life.

## PITIED LOVE.*

FAINTLY the sunset's sinking fires
Redden the waters, and above
Tip the gray oaken boughs like spires,
While, struggling like despair with love,

Are rustling shadows dropt with gold,
Deepening and nearing with the night,
Until at length they close, and fold
In their embrace the fainting light.

Up from the river blue mists curl,
The dew shines in the vale below,
And overhead, like beads of pearl,
The white buds of the mistletoe.

Lo! while the shade and light ingrain,
A dryad dweller of the tree,
Like the hushed murmur of soft pain,
Is pouring its sweet note for thee.

Lone one, beneath whose drooping head
The red leaves of the autumn lie,—

* The author acknowledges her indebtedness to Coleridge for one or two passages in this poem.

The winds have stooped to make that bed,
  O lonesome watcher of the sky!

Lifting his head a little up
  From the poor pillow where it lay,
And pushing from his forehead pale
  The long damp tresses all away:

He told me, with the eager haste
  Of one who dare not trust his words,
He knew a mortal with a voice
  As low and lovely as that bird's.

But that he saw once in a dell
  Separate from that a weary space,
A pale, meek lily, that as well
  Might woo that old oak's green embrace,

As for his heart to hope that she,
  Whose palace chamber ne'er grew dim,
Would leave the loves of royalty
  To wander through the world with him.

Once, leaping in a murderous cave
  He saved her from an outlaw band,
And with such tenderness she chid
  When twice he kissed her lily hand.

With the sweet burden as he flew,
  He dared to gaze upon her face,
And she forgave him, though he drew
  Closer and closer the embrace.

Why shook the fair form with alarm?
The proud Earl Say to meet her came,
And shrinking from that boyish arm,
Her cheek grew darkly red with shame!

And he, scarce knowing what he did,
But feeling that his heart was broke,
Fled from her pitying glance, and hid
In the cold shadows of that oak;

Where, as he said, she came at night
And clasped him from the bitter air,
With her soft arms of tender white,
And the dark beauty of her hair.

But when the morning lit the spray,
And hung its soft wreaths o'er his head,
The lovely lady passed away
Through mist of glory, pale and red.

So bitter grew his heaving sighs,
So mournful dark the glance he raised,
I looked upon him earnestly,
And saw the gentle boy was crazed!

How fair he was! it made me sad,
And soft as sad my bosom grew,
To think no earthly hand could build
That beautiful ruin up anew.

But pointing where the full moon's light
Lay redly on the village hills,

I told him that my hearth that night
  Was brighter:—How my bosom thrills,

Remembering how he hid his face
  In earth's cold bosom, cold and bare,
And told me of the warm embrace
  That meekly, sweetly kept him there.

Closer the dismal raven croaks—
  Flutters the wild-bird nigh and nigher—
A colder shadow than the oak's
  Has stilled that bosom's pulse of fire.

---

## ALONE BY THE TOMB.

WHERE solemn and heavy the shadow
  Of the old gray church is spread,
And the grass is crushed down and faded,
  I muse on the early dead.

Not the voiceless peace of my chamber,
  Nor the song, nor the hearth of light,
Nor the vistas of golden visions,
  Could quiet my soul to-night.

I would think of the meekness and beauty
  Of gentle and noiseless lives,

And not of the thwarted endeavour
  Of the spirit that hopes and strives.

Of the sweetness of household duty;
  Of the loves that never depart;
And not of the plummet of agony,
  Sounding the depths of the heart.

The starlight is dimly burning
  In the leaves, but the birds are still,
And no light gleams from the chambers,
  Narrow, and low, and chill.

I can hear the dull bat flitting,
  And the wind in the chancel moan—
O how can my feet walk firmly
  The valley of shade alone!

Sole friend of my heart, be with me
  In the time of the parting strife,
And read me the simple story
  Of the Cross, from the Book of Life.

'Twill strengthen me more than the greenness
  Of the rosied hills above,
To die on that pillow of beauty—
  The bosom of faithful love.

## TWO VISIONS.

I SAW a shadow through the sunshine pass,
  Bright and unsteady, but without a sound,
As a sleek serpent might divide the grass,
  Writhing and quivering with a mortal wound;
So came the thing, or shadow, nigh and nigher—
  But my eyes, weary with excess of pain,
Could tell not whether scales or sparks of fire
  Glistened and glinted on its tortuous train.

'Twas gone, and where it vanished from my view
  I saw a red and horrible mist arise,
And as it drifted thinly, straining through
  The fixed and ghastly shining of dead eyes.

And there were worms of shifting hues that lay
  Catching the radiance of the sinking sun,
As sick to dizzy death I turned away,
  Loosening a helm, close where a fountain run
There was a woman with pale wo distressed,
  'Neath her long tresses, damp with evening's breath,
Clasping a youth all softly, whose torn breast
  Was crimson with the bitter blood of death.

And as she looked upon him, her sweet eyes
  Grew moist with tenderer sorrow than might suit

The severance of worn and common ties;
But though her frail frame shook, her lips were mute.

He died, and rude men covered him away
From her embraces, with the common dust;
And though her cheek grew whiter than the spray
Of the vexed ocean, she forebore to trust
Her sorrow to the consonance of words;
But, weaving up his name with her sad song—
A broken warble like a wounded bird's—
She passed unconsciously the worshipping throng.

But of her sufferings the elaborate tale
Were a dark story that I cannot write;
Enough that in the thin grass of a vale
Quiet and lonesome, azure-leaved and white,
The violets are spreading o'er two graves,
One newer than the other. When the fold
Of a bright banner to wild music waves,
I think about those locks of paley gold,
Like the dissolving beam of a faint star;
And of the dying heart they clasped away
From the red shadow of the wing of war,
So strong of my strange vision is the sway.

There was a murmur through the shaken plumes
Of the green forest, and along the sea,
O'er the iced mountains, through the cavern glooms,
Touching the lost heart of humanity.
'Twas like the voice of a hair-girdled John
In the dim wilderness crying, Prepare the way,

That the blind children of men may look upon
  The shining glories of the risen day.

His cold dissecting-knife in Nature's breast,
  Unlocking the joints and laying the arteries bare,
Of hidden knowledge limited not the guest,
  But with their pale smile in his silver hair,
He cross-examined the stars, resolved the plans
  Of their far orbits, difficult and vast;
And in the charnel, loosening the bands,
  Wrenched the dark secrets from the unanswering past.
And when that soul of fire its aim had gained,
  Conning to wisdom even the martyr's blood,
With the soft links of love mankind were chained
  Into one universal brotherhood.

In the sweet pauses of the heart of prayer
  The air was full of music, meek as mild,
The light wind drifting back the golden hair
  From her white bosom, sat a little child;
And the wild warble of the morning bird
  Was hushed in its melodious throat, to trace
The windings of her song, while all who heard
  Pined for the beauty of her soft embrace.

Down to the stony floor of the blue sea
  Sunk the dim ghost of suffering and crime;
And he of the white tresses bent the knee
  In reverent worship of the type sublime.

## LOST DILLIE.

DON'T you remember the old apple-tree
 That grew in the edge of the meadow;
And the maiden whose thitherward straying with me
 Threw over the sward but one shadow?
Was it the blush of the apples that over us hung,
 Which threw o'er her cheek its soft splendour;
And the wild birds around us that lovingly sung,
 Which made her low warble so tender?

You remember the bridal-time, bright with the flow
 Of the cup as deceitful as cheery,
And the neat little cabin-home, always a-glow
 With the sweet smile of Dillie, my dearie!
When the wine smothered love's passionate flame,
 Her blue eyes drooped mournful and lowly;
How sadly she watched for the footstep that came
 Each night time more slowly and slowly!

The path going down to the apple-tree, still
 Winds over the slope of the meadow;
The dear little cabin peeps over the hill—
 But the roses run wild in its shadow!
Don't you remember the ivy-grown church
 We used to think lonesome and dreary?
Beneath the blue marble, just under the birch,
 Lies Dillie, lost Dillie, my dearie!

## PICTURES OF MEMORY.

Among the beautiful pictures
 That hang on Memory's wall,
Is one of a dim old forest,
 That seemeth best of all:
Not for its gnarled oaks olden,
 Dark with the mistletoe;
Not for the violets golden
 That sprinkle the vale below;
Not for the milk-white lilies
 That lead from the fragrant hedge,
Coquetting all day with the sunbeams,
 And stealing their golden edge;
Not for the vines on the upland
 Where the bright red berries rest,
Nor the pinks, nor the pale, sweet cowslip,
 It seemeth to me the best.

I once had a little brother,
 With eyes that were dark and deep—
In the lap of that old dim forest
 He lieth in peace asleep:
Light as the down of the thistle,
 Free as the winds that blow,
We roved there the beautiful summers,
 The summers of long ago;

But his feet on the hills grew weary,
And, one of the autumn eves,
I made for my little brother
A bed of the yellow leaves.

Sweetly his pale arms folded
My neck in a meek embrace,
As the light of immortal beauty
Silently covered his face:
And when the arrows of sunset
Lodged in the tree-tops bright,
He fell, in his saint-like beauty,
Asleep by the gates of light.
Therefore, of all the pictures
That hang on Memory's wall,
The one of the dim old forest
Seemeth the best of all.

---

## THE TWO MISSIONARIES.

In the pyramid's heavy shadows,
And by the Nile's deep flood,
They leaned on the arm of Jesus,
And preached to the multitude:
Where only the ostrich and parrot
Went by on the burning sands,
They builded to God an altar,
Lifting up holy hands.

But even while kneeling lowly
  At the foot of the cross to pray,
Eternity's shadows slowly
  Stole over their pilgrim way:
And one, with the journey weary,
  And faint with the spirit's strife,
Fell sweetly asleep in Jesus,
  Hard by the gates of life.

Oh, not in Gethsemane's garden,
  And not by Genesareth's wave,
The light, like a golden mantle,
  O'erspreadeth his lowly grave;
But the bird of the burning desert
  Goes by with a noiseless tread,
And the tent of the restless Arab
  Is silently near him spread.

Oh, could we remember only,
  Who shrink from the slightest ill,
His sorrows, who, bruised and lonely,
  Wrought on in the vineyard still—
Surely the tale of sorrow
  Would fall on the mourner's breast,
Hushing, like oil on the waters,
  The troubled wave to rest.

## LEILA.

Gone from us hast thou, in thy girlish hours,
What time the tenderest blooms of summer cease;
In thy young bosom bearing life's pale flowers
To the sweet city of eternal peace.

In the soft stops of silver singing rain,
Faint be the falling of the pale-rose light
O'er thy meek slumber, wrapt away from pain
In the fair robes of dainty bridal white.

Seven nights the stars have wandered through the blue,
Since thou to larger, holier life wert born;
And day as often, sandaled with gray dew,
Has trodden out the golden fires of morn.

Oft, ere the dim waves of the sea of wo
Clasp the green shore of immortality,
Life, like a planet cursed, lays down its glow,
And blindly wanders o'er immensity.

And, from thy starless passage and untried,
Faith shrank alarmed at feeble nature's cry;
Ere yet life's broken waves had multiplied
The intense radiance of eternity.

But now, on every sunbeam leaning bright
Across the white mists, trembling o'er the sea,
My soul goes forth, as on a path of light,
Questioning all things beautiful of thee.

Nor shall distrust or doubt my spirit move,
Doomed though it be the seal of wo to wear;
Since the blest memory of deathless love
Stands like a star between me and despair.

---

## THE HANDMAID.

Why rests a shadow on her woman's heart?
In life's more girlish hours it was not so;
Ill hath she learned to hide with harmless art
The soundings of the plummet-line of wo!

Oh what a world of tenderness looks through
The melting sapphire of her mournful eyes;
Less softly-moist are violets full of dew,
And the delicious colour of the skies.

Serenely amid worship doth she move,
Counting its passionate tenderness as dross;
And tempering the pleadings of earth's love,
In the still, solemn shadows of the cross.

It is not that her heart is cold or vain,
That thus she moves through many worshippers;

No step is lighter by the couch of pain,
   No hand on fever's brow lies soft as hers.

From the loose flowing of her amber hair
   The summer flowers we long ago unknit,
As something between joyance and despair
   Came in the chamber of her soul to sit.

In her white cheek the crimson burns as faint
   As red doth in some cold star's chastened beam;
The tender meekness of the pitying saint
   Lends all her life the beauty of a dream.

Thus doth she move among us day by day,
   Loving and loved; but passion cannot move
The young heart that has wrapped itself away
   In the soft mantle of a Saviour's love!

---

## THE POOR.

Cradled in poverty—unloved, alone,
   Seeing far off the wave of gladness roll;
Sorrow, to happier fortune never known,
   Strikes deep its poison-roots within the soul!

What need is there for rhetoric to seek
   For the fine phrase of eloquence, to tell
Of the eye sunken, and the hueless cheek,
   Where naked want and gnawing hunger dwell?

Down in the lanes and alleys of life's mart
Are beds of anguish that no kind hands tend;
And friendless wanderers, without map or chart,
Urged to despair, or, worse, a nameless end!

Their very smiles are bitter, in whose track
The fountains are with penury made chill;
For by their smiles, their sighs are driven back
To stifle in the heart-strings, and be still!

The poor are criminals! The opulent man
Is unsuspected, and must needs be true;
Such is the popular verdict, such the plan
That gives the loathsome hangman work to do!

If he who treads the convict's gloomy cell,
To soothe Heaven's vengeance with officious prayer,
Had dealt as kindly with him ere he fell,
Haply his presence had been needless there!

Oh there is need of union, firm and strong,
Of effort vigorous and directed well;
To rescue weakness from oppressive wrong
Would shake the deep foundations of dark hell!

Dear are the humble in God's equal sight,
And every hair upon their heads he sees,
Even as the laurel freshening in the light,
That trails along the path of centuries!

Then treat them kindly, for the selfsame hand,
(And with as large an exercise of power,)
That makes the planets in their order stand,
Gives its meek beauty to the desert flower.

## HEAVEN ON EARTH.

Oh, in this beautiful world I fain would deem
 Some things, at least, are what they seem to me;
That deepest joy is no ideal dream,
 Linking the thought to something yet to be.

That in the living present, we can find
 Enough to smooth the way beneath our feet,—
That where heart blends with heart and mind with mind,
 Even life's bitterest bitter hath a sweet!

I've dreamed of heaven—the full and perfect bliss
 That waits the spirit in a larger sphere;
And, looking up, have found enough in this
 To realize the rapturous vision here!

God hath made all things beautiful—the sky,
 The common earth, the sunshine, and the shade;
And with affections that can never die,
 Hath gifted every creature He hath made.

Oh they but mock us with a hollow lie,
 Who make this goodly land a vale of tears;
For if the soul hath immortality,
 This is the infancy of deathless years.

And if we live as God has given us power,
 Heaven is begun: no blind fatality
Can shut the living soul from its high dower
 Of shaping out a glorious destiny!

## FAR AWAY.

Far away, far away, there's a region of bliss
Too bright for our vision to view,
Though faintly its glories are mirrored in this,
As the light of the stars in the dew.

The loved and the loving of life's early day,
Who left us in sorrow and gloom,
Are all in that beautiful land, far away,
Where the roses are always in bloom.

'Tis true we have moments of bliss, even here,
But brief is the shadowless sky;
For hope, when the brightest, is mingled with fear,
And to live, is to know we must die.

The sunshine is followed by darkness and storm,
And friendship endures but a day,
And, oh ! while the kiss of devotion is warm,
The loved and the trusted betray.

How oft, when the bride with her garland is crown'd,
The roses are brought from the grave !
And the sunniest fountain that ever I found
Had the serpent concealed in its wave.

Then why should I mourn thee, lost friend of my soul?
Death cannot divide us for aye,
Though dark are the billows between us that roll,
We'll meet in that home far away.

## THE BETTER LAND.

KNOW ye the land where the roses and lilies
 Are bright on the hills, as the wing of a bird,—
Where down in the depths of the beautiful valleys
 The song of the worshipper always is heard?

'Tis up where they mourn not o'er time and its fleetness,
 But, free from the cumbering cries of the clod,
Their songs are the chains that in rapturous sweetness
 Link men to the angels, and angels to God!

Sometimes with the eve in her starry tiara
 And mantle of gold sitting down in the west,
Like echoes of harps from a far-away prairie,
 Faint melodies float from the land of the blest.

And sometimes, when sighing for one who would love me
 And share with me always in sadness or glee,
I see, from a soft island floating above me,
 A pale hand of beauty that beckons to me!

## FIRST LOVE.

FATHER of light, thy child recall,
She hath known of earthly bliss the all;
She hath loved and been beloved.—SCHILLER.

COME with me, dear one, from these haunted dells!
Still doth she linger, oh! so sad and meek;
Though joy no more her maiden bosom swells,
Nor kissing zephyr crimsons her white cheek.

In the cool shade of my delicious bower
This mournful whisper of the past shall cease;
There will I fold thee to my heart, pale flower;
Come, lovely trembler, give thyself to peace.

Sweet-throated birds with glowing wings are there,
Filling the woods with beauty all day long;
How softly thou wilt swim away from care,
Upon the charmèd wave of some blest song.

Faintly her young heart trembles, and the fringe
Lifts from the dewy wells of her clear eyes;
Her thin cheek deepens to a pale rose tinge—
And doth she love him? Hush! that look replies.

The golden tissue of love's web was crossed
With a dark sorrow, in this very vale;

Gone is the beautiful dream, its love-light lost,
  The winding sheet were scarcely now so pale.

And thy sweet, passionate pleading all is vain,
  Young wooer, of the eloquent lip and eye;
Her heart clings closer to its tender pain
  If joy but whisper; leave her, then, to die.

For still she lingers in this haunted spot,
  The light wind playing with her yellow hair,
And nestling to her cheek, she heeds it not;
  Then leave, oh! leave her—all *her* world is there!

---

## THE MILL-MAID.

Now comb her golden hair away;
  Meekly and sorrow-laden
She waited for the closing day—
  Poor broken-hearted maiden!
The ring from off her finger slip,
  And fold her hands together;
No more love's music on her lip
  Will tremble like a feather.

Each Sabbath-time along the aisle
  Her step more faintly sounded,
The light grew paler in her smile
  Her cheek less softly rounded;

But never sank we in despair
  Till with that fearful crying,
"The mill-maid of the golden hair
  And lily hand is dying!"

When the dim shadows of the birch
  Above her rest are swaying,
The pastor of the village church
  Shall bless the place with praying:
Deeming the voiceless sacrifice
  A loved and lovely blossom,
Blown by the winds of Paradise
  To Jesus' folding bosom.

The mill-wheel for a day is still,
  The spindle ceased its plying,
The little homestead on the hill
  Looks sadder for her dying;
But ere the third time in the spire
  The Sabbath bell is ringing,
Not one of all the village choir
  Will miss the mill-maid's singing.

## LOVE.

Nay, do not pity me, that not a star
Hangs in the bosom of my stormy sky,
Nor winglet of white feathers flutters by,
Nor like a soft dream swims or near or far
The golden atmosphere of poesy.
Down in the heart from frivolous joys aloof
Burn the pale fires, whose keen intensity
Flames through the web of life's discoloured woof,
And lights the white walls of eternity.
Alas! the ravishments of Love's sweet trust
May charm my life no more to passion's glow;
Nor the light kisses of a lip of dust
Crimson my forehead with the seal of wo;
Well, were it otherwise, 'tis better so!

## DEATH.

WITH your pale burden, gently, gently tread—
  She came to us a bride a year ago
  And now Love's sweet star crimsons the pale snow
About her early, melancholy bed.
Why weep ye for her? She hath done with pain,
  And meekly to our common portion bowed.
Unthread the roses from the shining train
  Of her long tresses, and prepare the shroud!
Her heart was full of dreams of heavenly birth,
  While in the borders of dim life she stayed,
  Like some young lily golden dews had weighed
Down to the chilly bosom of the earth:
  For but the wing of death, while here she trod,
  Rested between her beautiful life and God.

## THE CHARMED BIRD.

"MOTHER, oh, mother! this morning when Will
And Mary and I had gone out on the hill,
We stopped in the orchard to climb in the trees,
And broke off the blossoms that sweetened the breeze,
When right down before us, and close where we were,
There fluttered and fluttered a bird in the air.

"Its crest was so glossy, so bright were its eyes,
And its wings, oh! their colour was just like the skies;
And still as it chirped, and kept eddying round
In narrower circles and nearer the ground,
We looked, and all hid in the leaves of the brake,
We saw, don't you think, oh! the ugliest snake!"

Caressingly folding the child in her arms,
With thoughts of sweet birds in a world full of charms,
"My child," said the mother, "in life's later hours
Remember the morning you stopped for the flowers;
And still when you think of the bird in the air,
Forget not, my love, that the serpent was there."

# PRIDE.

THERE is a pride of heart, a damning pride,
  To which men sacrifice, that I detest;
And Peter-like, what thousands would have lied
  Even with profanation, or confessed
The Lord of glory with a burning cheek,
If Pilate and the Rulers heard them speak.

Man sees his weaker brother faint and die,
  And coldly passes on the other side;
Because within his bosom darkly lie
  The poisoned shadows of that Upas, pride,
Which, since from bliss the rebel angels fell,
Trail downward to the very gates of hell!

When, with the blushes burning on her cheek,
  And her dark locks unbound, the sinful came,
And humbly sat herself at Jesus' feet,
  Did he reproach her with her life of shame?
But for the many who aside have turned,
How hardly is that beautiful lesson learned!

## MISSIVE.

KNOW thou this truth, which the creeds cannot smother,
Wherever man is found, there is thy brother;
God his blest sire is, earth is his mother—
Where most degraded, thy zeal most increase;
Aid him and help him, till, ceasing to falter,
He shall come up to humanity's altar,
"Bearing white blocks for the city of Peace."

Shrink not away from the common and lowly—
Good deeds, though never so humble, are holy;
And though the recompense fall to thee slowly,
Heroes unnumbered before thee have trod;
By the sweet light of their blessed example,
Work on—the field of love's labour is ample—
Trusting Humanity, trusting in God!

Fight down the Wrong, howe'er specious its bearing,
Lighten the burdens about thee by sharing,
Fear not the glorious peril of daring,
Be it the rack or the prison's dull bars;
Hands are stretched out from the graves of past ages,
To brighten with holy deeds history's pages—
Martyr-fires burn as intensely as stars.

Never sit down by the wayside to sorrow—
Hope is a good angel, whence we may borrow
Beauty and gladness and light for the morrow,
   However dark be the present with ill;
And the far waves of Time's sorrowful river,
Wandering and weary and moaning for ever,
   Break on the rock of Eternity still.

---

## ONE DEPARTED.

Blest inspiration of unworthy song,
   A heart of tender sadness wooes thee back;
If in blind weakness I have done thee wrong,
   Accord me sweet forgiveness! Like the track
Of a bright bird, whereon soft notes are cast—
The time, the place is where I saw thee last!

Life has been weary with me since we met,
   Though in it moments of deep joy there lie,
Soft, as we see in cloud-rifts, cold and wet,
   Blue shifting patches of the summer sky:
For oft, thy gold locks wet with my salt tears,
Thy gentle semblance from the dust appears!

In the cold mists of morn, at evening soft,
   When odours make the winds so heavy-sweet,
Stretching my arms out, I have called thee oft,
   And night has heard the soundings of my feet

Where the blue slabs of marble, icy chill,
Keep in thy breast life's azure rivers still!

Like the faint dim vibrations of a lay
We sometimes half remember, half forget,
Thou, in the winding-sheet long wrapt away,
Troublest my heart with wildering beauty yet:
Nor have I ever met with mortal form
Sweet as thy shadow to my clasping arm!

Fade back to ashes, visitant divine,
Unutterably radiant as thou art,
If ever smile of dewy lip, save thine,
Hath touched the darkened ruins of my heart!
Thou wert in thy young life, and still dost seem,
The sweet and passionate music of a dream.

Sleep seals thy gentle eyes, but we are wed;
Thou wait'st my coming—shall I traitor prove
To the deep slumbers of the bridal bed,
And the birth-chamber of immortal love?
No! as the sweet rain visits the pale bloom,
I will come softly to thee in the tomb!

## MUSINGS BY THREE GRAVES.

THE dappled clouds are broken; bright and clear
   Comes up the broad and glorious star of day;
And night, the shadowy, like a hunted deer,
   Flies from the close pursuer fast away.

Now on my ear a murmur faintly swells,
   And now it gathers louder and more deep,
As the sweet music of the village bells
   Rouses the drowsy rustic from his sleep.

Hark! there's a footstep startling up the birds,
   And now as softly steals the breeze along;
I hear the sound, and almost catch the words
   Of the sweet fragment of a pensive song.

And yonder, in the clover-scented vale—
   Her bonnet in her hand, and simply clad—
I see the milkmaid with her flowing pail:
   Alas! what is it makes her song so sad?

In the seclusion of these lowly dells
   What mournful lesson has her bosom learned?
Is it the memory of sad farewells,
   Or faithless love, or friendship unreturned?

Methinks yon sunburnt swain, with knotted thong,
And rye-straw hat slouched careless on his brow,
Whistled more loudly, passing her along,
To yoke his patient oxen to the plough.

'Tis all in vain! she heeds not, if she hears,
And, sadly musing, separate ways they go,—
Oh, who shall tell how many bitter tears
Are mingled in the brightest fount below?

Poor, simple tenant of another's lands,
Vexed with no dream of heraldic renown;
No more the earnings of his sinewy hands
Shall make his spirit like the thistle's down.

Smile not, recipient of a happier fate,
And haply better formed life's ills to bear,
If e'er you pause to read the name and date
Of one who died the victim of despair.

Now morn is fully up; and while the dew
From off her golden locks is brightly shed,
In the deep shadows of the solemn yew,
I sit alone and muse above the dead.

Not with the blackbird whistling in the brake,
Nor when the rabbit lightly near them treads,
Shall they from their deep slumbering awake,
Who lie beneath me in their narrow beds.

Oh, what is life? at best a narrow bound,
  Where each that lives some baffled hope survives—
A search for something, never to be found,
  Records the history of the greatest lives!

There is a haven for each weary bark,
  A port where they who rest are free from sin;
But we, like children trembling in the dark,
  Drive on and on, afraid to enter in.

Here lies an aged patriarch at rest,
  To whom the needy never vainly cried,
Till in this vale, with toil and years oppressed,
  His long-sustaining staff was laid aside.

Oft for his country had he fought and bled,
  And gladly, when the lamp of life grew dim,
He joined the silent army of the dead—
  Then why should tears of sorrow flow for him?

We mourn not for the cornfield's deepening gold,
  Nor when the sickle on the hills is plied;
And wherefore should we sorrow for the old,
  Who perish when life's paths have all been tried?

How oft at noon, beneath the orchard trees,
  With brow serene and venerably fair,
I've seen a little prattler on his knees
  Smoothing with dimpled hand his silver hair.

When music floated on the sunny hills,
And trees and shrubs with opening flowers were drest,
She meekly put aside life's cup of ills,
And kindly neighbours laid her here to rest.

And ye who loved her, would ye call her back,
Where its deep thirst the soul may never slake;
And Sorrow, with her lean and hungry pack,
Pursues through every winding which we take?

Where lengthened years but teach the bitter truth
That transient preference does not make a friend;
That manhood disavows the love of youth,
And riper years of manhood, to the end.

Beneath this narrow heap of mouldering earth,
Hard by the mansions of the old and young,
A wife and mother sleeps, whose humble worth
And quiet virtues poet never sung.

With yonder cabin, half with ivy veiled,
And children by the hand of mercy sent,
And love's sweet star, that never, never paled,
Her bosom knew the fulness of content.

Mocking ambition never came to tear
The finest fibres from her heart away,—
The aim of her existence was to bear
The cross in patient meekness day by day.

No hopeless, blind idolater of chance,
  The sport and plaything of each wind that blows,
But lifting still by faith a heavenward glance,
  She saw the waves of death around her close.

And here her children come with pious tears,
  And strew their simple offerings in the sod;
And learn to tread like her the vale of years,
  Beloved of man, and reconciled to God.

Now from the village school the urchins come,
  And shout and laughter echo far and wide;
The blue smoke curls from many a rustic home,
  Where all their simple wants are well supplied.

The laboured hedger, pausing by the way,
  Picks the ripe berries from the gadding vine:
The axe is still, the cattle homeward stray,
  And transient glories mark the day's decline.

## TO THE EVENING ZEPHYR.

I SIT where the wild bee is humming,
And listen in vain for thy song;
I've waited before for thy coming,
But never, oh! never so long.

How oft, with the blue sky above us,
And waves breaking light on the shore,
Thou, knowing they would not reprove us,
Hast kissed me a thousand times o'er!

So sweet were thy dewy embraces,
Thy falsity who could believe!
Some phantom thy fondness effaces—
Thou couldst not have aimed to deceive?

Thou *toldest* thy love for me never,
But all the bright stars in the skies,
Though striving to do so for ever,
Could scarcely have numbered thy sighs.

Alone in the gathering shadows,
Still waiting, sweet Zephyr, for thee,
I look for the waves of the meadows,
And dimples to dot the blue sea.

The blossoms that waited to greet thee
  With heat of the noontide opprest,
Now flutter so lightly to meet thee,
  Thou'rt coming, I know, from the West.

Alas! if thou findest me pouting,
  'Tis only my love that alarms;
Forgive, then, I pray thee, my doubting,
  And take me once more to thy arms!

## Answer.

BY MAJOR G. W. PATTEN, U. S. A.

Oh! sweet as the prayer of devotion
  Comes thy song, fair enchantress, to me;
And cleaving through mists of the ocean
  I quicken my pinions for thee.

I know that no day-breeze has dallied
  Unreproved, with thy ringlets of jet,
Since the moon when so gayly I sallied
  From thy lips with my dew kisses wet.

That I love thee, I cannot dissemble—
  I would not if even I might;
At thy touch doth my light pinion tremble,
  And my voice murmurs low at thy sight

Though born for the pathways of heaven,
My wing ever shadows the lea,
If I rise with the light clouds of even,
I soar but to wander to *thee.*

I've sported in evergreen bowers
With blossoms sweet-scented and gay,
And I've toyed, mid those beautiful flowers,
With beings as peerless as they:

But naught did I ever discover,
Whose nature seemed nearer divine,
Than the lip of my warm-hearted lover
When its kisses are mingled with mine.

Then no more "where the wild bee is humming,"
Stay to "sit" and to "listen in vain;"
I shall come—even now am I coming,
To fondle and fan thee again.

## Response.

O'ER clouds of carnation and amber
Shone faintly the first gentle star,
As I caught from the hush of my chamber
Thy answering song from afar.

If false, thou hast sweetly dissembled,
Light spirit of mountain and sea,

And I—how my glad bosom trembled
At even that whisper from thee!

Stoop down if thou wilt, breezy rover,
To the blossoms thy pathway along,
But lightly, my dewy-lipped lover,
And oh! sing them not such a song.

For never an elfin nor fairy,
Nor warbler with wing on the sky,
Nor white-bosomed bird of the prairie
Could love thee so fondly as I.

Not a moment the day-breeze has trifled
"Unreproved with my ringlets of jet,"
Since the moon when my fond heart was rifled,
The moon when as lovers we met.

Chanting over thy song of devotion,
I'll watch from the hill-tops each day,
For the path through the white mists of ocean
Where thy pinion is cleaving its way.

Till the last summer-bee ceases humming—
The last bird goes over the sea,
Since thou sayst, "I will come, I am coming,"
I'll wait, my sweet Zephyr, for thee!

## THE SAILOR'S STORY.

NIGHT is falling, clouds are sweeping,
And, ere morning, there may be
Many a brother sailor sleeping
In the white arms of the sea.

But with courage tempest-daring,
Hearts through all things true and warm,
Warily our vessel wearing,
We may weather out the storm.

And, as o'er each other rising,
Billows sweep our deck, as then,
Even as impulses of sorrow
Cross the souls of wicked men;

Listen, comrades, to a story
Which the night with hope may arm—
Heaven's soft rainbow, dropt with glory,
Hangs its beauty o'er the storm.

In the shadows of dark sorrow,
By the river of wild wo,
Once there was a weary mortal
Ever wandering to and fro.

Ever wandering, ever gazing,
Half in love and half in dread,
On the blue and sunken hollows
Of that wretched river's bed.

For, within those grayish caverns,
With each billow's fall and rise,
Coils of green and yellow serpents
Lifted up their hungry eyes.

Sadly dwelt he, wrapt from sunshine,
With a right hand maimed and dumb,
Crying often at the noontide,
"Will the morning never come?"

Once a sailor, lost, benighted,
Drifting on the whirlpool's rim,
Shouted for the help that came not—
Messmates, think you that was him?

With his long locks, briny, tangled,
Clasping a torn bosom round,
Washed upon the cold, wet sand-beach,
Once a dying man was found;

Where the plumes of pale-pink sea-weed
Drifted like a sunset cloud,
And the mists of wo's wild river
Hung about him like a shroud.

Morning, like a woman, clasped him
  With her hair, a golden train,
And kissed back the living crimson
  To his pallid cheek again.

But, as near that solemn river
  Wearily and slow he trod,
Pitying eye of mortal never
  Rested on that child of God.

So the burning of roused hatred
  In his heart dried up the dew,
And the very milk of kindness
  Bitter in its fountain grew.

But with light upon their bosoms
  Burning, burning evermore,
Birds that nested in the blossoms
  Haunted that wild river-shore—

Telling their sweet-throated story,
  From their morning beds of dew,
Upward, on their wings of glory,
  Farther, farther as they flew.

From that heart, despised, despising,
  Went a yearning for their song,
Like the sorrowful uprising
  Of a passion smothered long.

As through waves of light uplifted
  On and on he saw them swim,
He forgot the boat that drifted,
  Helpless, on the whirlpool's rim.

And his thoughts, like winged swallows
  From their dark home, rise and rise
O'er that river's sunken hollows,
  Shining with the hungry eyes.

Plunging in, like a Leander
  With a heart on fire, he flew,
And the waves before him parted,
  Like a mist of sun and dew.

Once, a steed with smoking haunches,
  And his loose mane streaming back,
To the rider's light caresses
  Bounded on a pathless track.

With his glossy neck strained forward,
  And an eye of ocean blue,
Through the ringing, moonlit forest
  Like an ebon shaft he flew.

Like the wild mane of the courser
  Flowing on the wind upborne,
Went the wild song of the rider,
  Flowing from a lip unshorn.

Something of a wretched river
  Dimly moaning far behind,
And of birds with burning bosoms,
  Was that music on the wind.

Pushing back a cloud of ringlets
  Bound with blossoms pale as snow,
Softly blushing, fondly gazing
  Toward the line of woods below;

Waited in her bridal chamber
  One whose faith was never dim—
Eager horseman—frighted bosom,
  Dost thou tremble so for him?

---

## A LOCK OF HAIR.

Three times the zephyr's whisper,
  And the soft sunlit showers,
Have called up from their slumber
  The early spring-time flowers,—

Three times the Summer wild-birds
  Have built among the trees,
And gone with the dull Autumn
  Three times across the seas,—

Since this bright lock was severed
  In the hopelessness of bliss:
O, there's a world of eloquence
  In simple things like this!

What a tumult of strange feelings
  It wakes within my brain;
Half joyous and half sorrowful—
  Half rapture, half of pain.

One moment I am dreaming
  Love's broken chain is whole,
And echoes of lost music
  Are trembling in my soul.

Another, and I'm sitting
  Where the lights of memory burn,
And thinking of the summer-times
  That never can return.

Oft in the solemn watches
  Of the long and weary night,
No link beside has bound me
  To the morning and the light.

'Tis strange my heart will vibrate
  From gladness to despair,
Whenever I am thinking of
  This simple tress of hair.

## VISIONS OF LIGHT.

THE moon is rising in beauty,
 The sky is solemn and bright,
And the waters are singing like lovers
 That walk in the valleys at night.

Like the towers of an ancient city,
 That darken against the sky,
Seems the blue mist of the river
 O'er the hill-tops far and high.

I see through the gathering darkness
 The spire of the village church,
And the pale white tombs, half hidden
 By the tasselled willow and birch.

Vain is the golden drifting
 Of morning light on the hill;
No white hands open the windows
 Of those chambers low and still.

But their dwellers were all my kindred,
 Whatever their lives might be,
And their sufferings and achievements
 Have recorded lessons for me.

Not one of the countless voyagers
 Of life's mysterious main

Has laid down his burden of sorrows,
   Who hath lived and loved in vain.

From the bards of the elder ages
   Fragments of song float by,
Like flowers in the streams of summer,
   Or stars in the midnight sky.

Some plumes in the dust are scattered,
   Where the eagles of Persia flew,
And wisdom is reaped from the furrows
   The plough of the Roman drew.

From the white tents of the Crusaders
   The phantoms of glory are gone,
But the zeal of the barefooted hermit
   In humanity's heart lives on.

Oh! sweet as the bell of the Sabbath
   In the tower of the village church,
Or the fall of the yellow moonbeams
   In the tasselled willow and birch—

Comes a thought of the blessed issues
   That shall follow our social strife,
When the spirit of love maketh perfect
   The beautiful mission of life:

For visions of light are gathered
   In the sunshine of flowery nooks,
Like the shades of the ghostly Fathers
   In their twilight cells of books!

## A LEGEND OF ST. MARY'S.

ONE night, when bitterer winds than ours,
  On hill-sides and in valleys low,
Built sepulchres for the dead flowers,
  And buried them in sheets of snow,—

When over ledges dark and cold,
  The sweet moon, rising high and higher,
Tipped with a dimly burning gold
  St. Mary's old cathedral spire,—

The lamp of the confessional,
  (God grant it did not burn in vain,)
After the solemn midnight bell,
  Streamed redly through the lattice-pane.

And kneeling at the father's feet,
  Whose long and venerable hairs,
Now whiter than the mountain sleet,
  Could not have numbered half his prayers,

Was one—I cannot picture true
  The cherub beauty of his guise;
Lilies, and waves of deepest blue,
  Were something like his hands and eyes!

Like yellow mosses on the rocks,
Dashed with the ocean's milk-white spray,
The softness of his golden locks
About his cheek and forehead lay.

Father, thy tresses, silver-sleet,
Ne'er swept above a form so fair;
Surely the flowers beneath his feet
Have been a rosary of prayer!

We know not, and we cannot know,
Why swam those meek blue eyes with tears;
But surely guilt, or guiltless wo,
Had bowed him earthward more than years.

All the long summer that was gone,
A cottage maid, the village pride,
Fainter and fainter smiles had worn,
And on that very night she died!

As soft the yellow moonbeams streamed
Across her bosom, snowy fair,
She said, (the watchers thought she dreamed,)
"'Tis like the shadow of his hair!"

And they could hear, who nearest came,
The cross to sign and hope to lend,
The murmur of another name
Than that of mother, brother, friend.

An hour—and St. Mary's spires,
Like spikes of flame, no longer glow—

No longer the confessional fires
  Shine redly on the drifted snow.

An hour—and the saints had claimed
  That cottage maid, the village pride;
And he, whose name in death she named,
  Was darkly weeping by her side.

White as a spray-wreath lay her brow
  Beneath the midnight of her hair,
But all those passionate kisses now
  Wake not the faintest crimson there!

Pride, honour, manhood, cannot check
  The vehemence of love's despair—
No soft hand steals about his neck,
  Or bathes its beauty in his hair!

Almost upon the cabin walls
  Wherein the sweet young maiden died,
The shadow of a castle falls,
  Where for her young lord waits a bride!

With clear blue eyes and flaxen hair,
  In her high turret still she sits;
But, ah! what scorn her ripe lips wear—
  What shadow to her bosom flits!

From that low cabin tapers flash,
  And, by the shimmering light they spread,
She sees beneath its mountain ash,
  Leafless, but all with berries red,

Impatient of the unclasped rein,
  A courser that should not be there—
The silver whiteness of his mane
  Streaming like moonlight on the air!

Oh, Love! thou art avenged too well—
  The young heart, broken and betrayed,
Where thou didst meekly, sweetly dwell,
  For all its sufferings is repaid.

Not the proud beauty, nor the frown
  Of her who shares the living years,
From her the winding-sheet wraps down,
  Can ever buy away the tears!

---

## THE NOVICE OF ST. MARY'S.

FROM "THE MONASTERY" OF SIR WALTER SCOTT.

Dark in the shade of the mountains,
  From a valley full of flowers,
Rose up, in the light of the setting sun,
  St. Mary's chapel towers.

The bell of the old gray turret
  Was tolling deep and slow,
And friars were telling their beads, and monks
  Chanting their hymns below.

But the breath of the silver censers,
  As they swung in the twilight dim,
And the sacred hush as the beads were told,
  And the chant of the solemn hymn;

And the golden light of the sunset
  Might bear to the heart no joy,
Of one whose mantle of coarsest serge
  Betokened a novice boy.

Pale was his brow, and dreamy,
  And his bright locks yet unshorn:
He had but given his mother's smile
  For the convent's gloom that morn.

O, why are his pale hands folded
  In the chill of the cloister's gloom?
Why loses his cheek its roundness,
  And his lip its rosy bloom?

Let Mary of Avenel answer,
  As she sits in the twilight dim,
In the leafy shade of her garden bower—
  Does she wait for the convent hymn?

No, her young heart softly trembles
  From its even pulse of joy,
As she hears a step, but 'tis not the step
  Of St. Mary's Novice Boy!

## HELVA.

HER white hands full of mountain flowers,
Down by the rough rocks and the sea,
Helva, the raven-tressed, for hours,
Hath gazed forth earnestly.

Unconscious that the salt spray flecks
The ebon beauty of her hair—
What vision is it she expects,
So meekly lingering there?

Is it to see the sea-fog lift
From the broad bases of the hills,
Or the red moonlight's golden drift,
That her soft bosom thrills?

Or yet to see the starry hours
Their silver network round her throw,
That 'neath the white hands, full of flowers,
Her heart heaves to and fro?

Why strains so far the aching eye?
Kind nature wears to-night no frown,
And the still beauty of the sky
Keeps the mad ocean down.

Why are those damp and heavy locks
Put back, the faintest sound to win?
Ah! where the beacon lights the rocks,
A ship is riding in!

Who comes forth to the vessel's side,
Leaning upon the manly arm
Of one who wraps with tender pride
The mantle round her form?

Oh, Helva, watcher of lone hours,
May God in mercy give thee aid!
Thy cheek is whiter than thy flowers—
Thy woman's heart betrayed!

---

## THE TIME TO BE.

I SIT where the leaves of the maple
And the gnarled and the knotted gum
Are circling and drifting around me,
And think of the time to come.

For the human heart is the mirror
Of the things that are near and far;
Like the wave that reflects in its bosom
The flower and the distant star.

And beautiful to my vision
Is the time it prophetically sees,

As was once to the monarch of Persia
  The gem of the Cycladés.

As change is the order of Nature,
  And beauty springs from decay,
So in its destined season
  The false for the true makes way.

The darkening power of evil,
  And discordant jars and crime,
Are the cry preparing the wilderness
  For the flower and the harvest-time.

Though doubtings and weak misgivings
  May rise to the soul's alarm,
Like the ghosts of the heretic burners,
  In the province of bold Reform.

And now as the summer is fading,
  And the cold clouds full of rain,
And the net, in the fields of stubble
  And the briers, is spread in vain—

I catch, through the mists of life's river,
  A glimpse of the time to be,
When the chain from the bondman rusted,
  Shall leave him erect and free—

On the solid and broad foundation,
  A common humanity's right,
To cover his branded shoulder
  With the garment of love from sight.

## ELOQUENCE.

LIKEST the first Apostle,
Fearless of scoffs he stood,
Preaching Christ and the resurrection
To the eager multitude.

The light on his broad clear forehead
Fell not from the gorgeous pane,
As he spoke of the blessed Jesus,
Who died, and is risen again.

How beautiful on the mountains
The feet of the righteous are;
How sweet is the silver singing
Of lips that are used to prayer.

Will the rain of the dull, cold autumn
Awaken the sleeping flower?
Or the heart of the sinful soften,
Though the godless preach with power?

But the light of the golden summer
Will ripen the harvest grain,
And words that are fitly spoken
Will meet a response again.

And the hearts of a thousand bosoms
  Shrank frightened and trembling back,
Like a fawn in a heath of blossoms,
  With the hunters on its track.

For they heard, as the full tone deepened
  To eloquence sublime,
Echoes of muffled footsteps
  In the corridors of crime;

And saw the low-voiced Tempter
  Thence lure the weak to die,
As the bird in narrowing circles
  Goes down to the serpent's eye.

But when of Heaven's sweet mercy,
  He bade them not despair;
Bright through the vaulted temple
  Floated the wings of prayer.

As home I journeyed slowly
  From the multitude apart,
Messengers good and holy
  Kept knocking at my heart.

When sleep descended brightly,
  I heard the anthem's roll,
And all night my heart beat lightly
  To the music in my soul.

## TO ELMA.

How heavily the sea-waves break!
The storm wails loud and deep;
Wake, sister, from thy slumber wake,
For, oh! I cannot sleep.

My head is resting on thine arm,
Thy heart beats close to mine;
But, oh! this weary night of storm—
How can such peace be thine?

Thou answerest not—again I hear
Thy breathing, calm and deep;
No sorrow hast thou, and no fear—
I wish that I could sleep!

They tell of warning lights that gleam,
And ghosts such nights that glide,
And dreams—ay, once I had a dream—
'Tis more than verified!

Louder against the flinty sand
I hear the dashing seas;
No angel holds my trembling hand
Such fearful nights as these.

Why strive to cheat myself, or hark
  To hear the tempest laid?
'Tis not the storm, and not the dark,
  That makes my heart afraid!

For if my ear, in tempest strife,
  Is quickened to its roll,
'Tis that the promise of my life
  Is broken in my soul.

Yet speak to me! and lay thy hand
  Upon my aching brow—
I've nothing on the sea or land
  To love or cling to now!

---

## TO FLORA.

Away with regal palaces
  And diadems of gold:
There's nothing in the world so sweet
  As love's embracing fold.

I care not if the sea be rough
  And if the sky be dark,
If thou, beloved of my soul,
  Art with me in the bark.

Blest inspiration of my song!
I would not leave thy side,
To wear the stars of royalty,
And be a monarch's bride.

May thy fond arms encircle me
As time goes smoothly by,
And may thy faithful bosom be
My pillow when I die.

The time to come with flowers we'll sow
As all the past has been,
And though our cabin may be low,
The angels will come in.

If bitterness our cup should fill
And evil angels send,
Oh! what a sweetener of the ill
To know we have a friend.

Of Heaven above I ask but this
Of happiness conferred—
One heart that feels diviner bliss
Whene'er my step is heard.

## MYRRHA.

I'M thinking, my sweet Myrrha,
  Of that happy time in youth,
When all the world appeared like thee,
  In innocence and truth.

Oh! when around the shining hearth,
  At night, we used to meet,
There was music in the treading
  Of the little naked feet.

And I am thinking, Myrrha,
  Of the smiles and kindly words,
That ever lulled us to our sleep,
  And called us with the birds.

I think, until it almost seems
  The kiss is on my brow;—
Alas! 'tis only in my dreams;
  I have no mother now!

I am thinking of the Sabbath,
  When, alone and sad, I trod
A path each day is wearing down
  More deeply in the sod.

Sometimes, I have been happy since,
  And trust I yet shall be;
But never, sister of my soul!
  Have I forgotten thee.

## TO MYRRHA.

The love where Death has set his seal,
Nor age can chill nor rival steal,
Nor falsehood disavow.—BYRON.

YES, the living cast me from them,
As the rock the clasping wave;
Once there was one who loved me—
She is buried in the grave.

In the play-haunts of my childhood,
She was always by my side;
Oh! she loved me in her lifetime,
And she loved me when she died.

God knoweth my dark sorrow
When I knew that all was o'er,
And called her every lovely name,
But she could speak no more.

I could not, dare not, look upon
The strife, the parting dread;
But my heart I felt was breaking,
And I knew that she was dead.

They told me she was passing
Through the golden gates of day,

When the hand that meekly clasped my neck
  Fell heavily away.

I forgot the harp of Gabriel,
  The glory of the crown—
When the foldings of the winding-sheet
  Had wrapt her still heart down.

Shall I gather back my broken hopes
  From her cold sepulchre?
No! none have loved me in their lives
  Or in their deaths like her.

---

## TO THE SPIRIT OF TRUTH.

Bright-winged spirit of the sky,
  Beautiful and holy,
Pass thou not, neglectful by
  The despised and lowly.

Where the mourner by the tomb
  Sits, the dark unheeding,
With the white down of thy plume
  Bind the heart from bleeding.

Like the sweet light of the stars,
  Pierce the gloomiest prison,

Leaving broken bolts and bars
Cerements of the risen.

Where along the furrowed soil
Corn and rice are springing,
Let us hear the child of toil
At his labour singing.

Though the downy lip of youth
Whiten with vain terror,
With thy sacred wand, O Truth!
Smite gray-bearded Error.

Right in Superstition's frown
Be his doom allotted,
And to lower the coffin down,
Hangman's cords be knotted.

Where the progeny of sin
Hold their horrid revels,
In the Master's name go in,
And rebuke the devils.

Surely the "good time" is nigh
For thy wide diffusion;
Else God's promise is a lie,
And our faith, delusion.

## TO ———.

HAPLY beneath heaven's equal beams
  There lies some green and peaceful isle,
Where, gathering up my broken dreams,
  I yet may smile, or seem to smile.
Away, false hope, nor blind my eyes;
  I feel, I know my doom of ill;
Unbind thy web of hollow lies,
  And let my heart bleed as it will.

I know that I am changed—that years
  Have left their shadows on my brow,
And the dim traces of some tears—
  But these to thee are nothing now.
I'm sitting on the mossy stone,
  Where we have talked of love till death,
And thinking, but alone, *alone*,
  And thou—ah! who has broken faith?

I will not tell thee not to go,
  Nor ask thee yet to think of me;
My doom of dark and hopeless wo
  Has been too much entwined with thee.
For if thou seest, from me apart,
  A sunnier path than both have known,
I'll fold the darkness to my heart,
  And sit, as now, alone, alone.

## THE TWO LOVERS.

SINGING down a quiet valley,
Singing to herself she went,
And, with wing aslant, the zephyr
To her cheek with kisses leant.

Dainty, with the golden blossoms
Of the mulberries' silver braid,
Were the windings of the valley
Where the singing maiden strayed.

Where the river mist was climbing
Thin and white along the rocks,
On a hollow reed sat piping,
Like a shepherd to his flocks,

One whose lip was scarcely darkened
With the dawn of manhood's pride,
With his earnest eyes bent downward
To the river's voiceless tide.

Answering to his pleading music
Smiled a lovelit, girlish face,
Folded by the placid waters
In their chilly, cold embrace.

Like the summer sunshine parted
By the white wing of a dove,
Like the mist that sweetly trembles
Round the pensive star of love;

Were the pale and wavy ringlets
Drifting on the pearly tide,
While the music, wilder, deeper,
On the hushed air rose and died.

Treading down the golden blossoms
Of the mulberries' silver braid,
Struck a steed, with lordly rider,
Toward the half enchanted maid.

Like a rose-cloud from the sunset,
Like the love-light from a dream,
Fled the wildering shade of beauty
From the bosom of the stream.

Haunted by the cherub shadow
He could woo not from the wave,
Day by day the boy grew sadder,
And went pining to the grave.

Singing down the quiet valley,
Singing as the day grows dim,
Walks the maiden, but her visions
Blend not with a thought of him!

## ABJURATION.

HAUNTING phantom, I abjure thee!
Thou shalt never vex me more;
Though the past was sweet as summer,
Better far to look before.

Who would sit in memory's chambers,
Mantled from the loving light;
With the sea of life before them,
Broad, and beautiful, and bright?

Wherefore in the port of sorrow
Should our moorings longer be?
Helmsman, ho! heave up the anchor!
Now, my messmates, for the sea!

Up, my chamois-footed reefer!
Let the canvas be unfurled—
Moth will fret away the garment
Faster than the wearing world!

Though our bark is not too steady,
And our compass sometimes errs,
Never let the sail be slackened—
Storms make skilful mariners:

True, beneath these waves of beauty,
  Far from wind and tempest-frown,
When the sky was full of sunshine
  Many vessels have gone down.

Happiness is not in wooing
  Phantoms to the vacant breast;
But in earnest, healthful striving,
  And in blessing we are blest.

Are we ready? are we freighted?
  Not with odours, not with gold;
But with bright hopes for the future—
  With true hearts and courage bold!

Downward from the shore of sorrow
  Fresh the seaward breezes spring;
And our flag is up and waving,
  Like some proud bird's open wing.

When the showers of evening crimson
  Fall like roses on the sea;
Rocking o'er the glad, free billows,
  Oh, how sweet my dreams will be!

## OLD STORIES.

No beautiful star will twinkle
  To-night through my window-pane,
As I list to the mournful falling
  Of the leaves and the autumn rain.

High up in his leafy covert
  The squirrel a shelter hath;
And the tall grass hides the rabbit,
  Asleep in the churchyard path.

On the hills is a voice of wailing
  For the pale dead flowers again,
That sounds like the heavy trailing
  Of robes in a funeral train.

Oh, if there were one who loved me—
  A kindly and gray-haired sire,
To sit and rehearse old stories
  To-night by my cabin fire:

The winds as they would might rattle
  The boughs of the ancient trees—
In the tale of a stirring battle
  My heart would forget all these.

Or if, by the embers dying,
We talked of the past, the while,
I should see bright spirits flying
From the pyramids and the Nile.

Echoes from harps long silent
Would troop through the aisles of time,
And rest on the soul like sunshine,
If we talked of the bards sublime.

But, hark! did a phantom call me,
Or was it the wind went by?
Wild are my thoughts and restless,
But they have no power to fly.

In place of the cricket humming,
And the moth by the candle's light,
I hear but the deathwatch drumming—
I've heard it the livelong night.

Oh for a friend who loved me—
Oh for a gray-haired sire,
To sit with a quaint old story
To-night by my cabin fire.

## SPECTRES.

ONCE more the shadows darken
Upon life's solemn stream—
Once more I'm in my chamber
To ponder and to dream.

Down in the mist-white valley,
Across the hills afar,
The rosy light is gleaming
From Love's descending star.

I hear from yonder parlour
A prattler cry, "He's come!"
Oh, there's a world of comfort—
I wish *I* had a home!

All last night, round about me
The lights of memory streamed,
And my heart to long-lost music
Kept beating as I dreamed.

We live with spectres haunted
That we cannot exorcise—
A pale and shadowy army
Between us and the skies.

Conjured by mortal weakness,
  In their cerements they start
From the lonesome burial-places
  Of the dead hopes of the heart.

They will meet thee, fellow-pilgrim,
  For their graves are everywhere,
And thou canst not lay them better
  Than by labour which is prayer.

---

## LUCIFER.

Usurper of the throne of God,
  From heaven's high battlement cast down,
What spot of earth hast thou not trod,
  Wearing rebellion as a crown?

Like some bright meteor of the air
  Streams o'er the world thy robe of flame;
Ruined, fallen, yet as angel fair,
  I breathe my curses on thy name!

The broad road going down to death,
  What thousands but for thee would quit,
And climb to the green hills of faith,
  From the black ashes of the pit.

Once, when through Mercy's gates, ajar,
  I heard salvation's anthem flow,
Thy fire-wing led me, like a star,
  Back to the wretched gates of wo!

O, Holy Spirit, cease to grieve
  That slighted offer of thy grace;
My heart is breaking to receive
  The beauty of thy sweet embrace.

I cannot, will not let thee go,
  Has been my cry—nor shall it cease,
Till the wild billows of my wo
  Shall bear me to the shore of peace.

Go, lay thy forehead in hell's coals,
  Proud scorner of the bended knee,
For broken faith and perjured souls
  Charged all their awful guilt to thee.

And when at last the quick and dead
  Are summoned to the judgment bar,
If there shall be a crime more dread
  Than all the rest, to answer for—

Thine is it; for no evil hand,
  Save that which opened first the grave,
Could ever sink the accursed brand
  In the crouched shoulder of the slave.

## BE ACTIVE.

THOU who silently art weeping,
  Thou of faded lip and brow,
Golden harvests for thy reaping
  Wave before thee even now.

Fortune may be false and fickle—
  Should you, therefore, pause and weep?
Taking in thy hand the sickle,
  Enter in the field, and reap.

Though the garden, famed Elysian,
  May be shut from thee by fate,
Thou hast yet a holier mission
  Than to linger at the gate.

When so oft the rosiest morning
  Slumbers in the tempest's arms,
Should the cloud of dismal warning
  Fill the soul with vague alarms:

Brightest visions from thy pillow
  May have vanished, still thou'rt blest,
While the waves of time's rough billows
  Wash the shores of endless rest.

Should the powers of darkness blind thee,
  Should their whispers fill thy heart,
Say thou, Satan, get behind me!
  And the tempter will depart.

Then, to every fortune equal,
  Let us combat to the last,
That life's marches in the sequel
  May retrieve the wasted past.

---

## DEATH'S FERRYMAN.

Boatman, thrice I've called thee o'er,
Waiting on life's solemn shore,
Tracing, in the silver sand,
Letters till thy boat should land.

Drifting out alone with thee,
Toward the clime I cannot see,
Read to me the strange device
Graven on thy wand of ice.

Push the curls of golden hue
From thy eyes of starlit dew,
And behold me where I stand,
Beckoning thy boat to land.

Where the river mist, so pale,
Trembles like a bridal veil,
O'er yon lowly drooping tree,
One that loves me waits for me.

Hear, sweet boatman, hear my call!
Last year, with the leaflet's fall,
Resting her pale hand in mine,
Crossed she in that boat of thine.

When the corn shall cease to grow,
And the rye-field's silver flow
At the reaper's feet is laid,
Crossing, spake the gentle maid:

Dearest love, another year
Thou shalt meet this boatman here—
The white fingers of despair
Playing with his golden hair.

From this silver-sanded shore,
Beckon him to row thee o'er;
Where yon solemn shadows be,
I shall wait thee—come and see!

There! the white sails float and flow,
One in heaven and one below;
And I hear a low voice cry,
Ferryman of Death am I.

## WATCHING.

Thy smile is sad, Elella,
 Too sad for thee to wear,
For scarcely have we yet untwined
 The rosebuds from thy hair.

So, dear one, hush thy sobbing,
 And let thy tears be dried—
Methinks thou shouldst be happier,
 Three little months a bride.

Hark; how the winds are heaping
 The snow-drifts cold and white—
The clouds like spectres cross the sky—
 Oh, what a lonesome night!

The hour grows late and later,
 I hear the midnight chime:
Thy heart's fond keeper, where is he?
 Why comes he not?—'tis time!

Here make my heart thy pillow,
 And, if the hours seem long,
I'll while them with a legend wild,
 Or fragment of old song—

Or read, if that will soothe thee,
  Some poet's pleasant rhymes :
Oh, I have watched and waited thus,
  I cannot tell the times !

Hush, hark ! across the neighbouring hills
  I hear the watch-dog bay—
Stir up the fire, and trim the lamp,
  I'm sure he's on the way.

Could that have only been the winds,
  So like a footstep near ?
No, smile, Elella, smile again,
  He's coming home—he's here !

## ON THE DEATH OF A CHILD.

VAIN it were to say that night
Folds away the morrow—
Oh, you cannot see the light
Through this aching sorrow!

Beauty from your lives is borne,
Brother, sister, weeping;
But the cherub boy you mourn
Is not dead, but sleeping.

Folded are the dimpled arms
From your soft caressing;
Yet our God in darker forms
Sendeth down his blessing.

Death, a breeze from heaven astray,
Still, with wing the fleetest,
Drifts the lovely flowers away,
Where hope clings the sweetest.

Strong to change, but not destroy,
While the paley winglets
Veil the forehead of the boy
Bright with golden ringlets.

Faith, though dumb at the great loss
  Which hath made you weepers,
Closer, closer clasps the Cross
  Down among the sleepers.

And though wild your anguish be,
  And your hearts all broken,
"Suffer them to come to me,"
  Hath been sweetly spoken.

---

## CRADLE SONG.

WEARY of the mother's part?
  My sweet baby, never!
I will rock thee on my heart
  Ever, yes, for ever!

Loveliest of lovely things
  Pure as the evangel!—
O, in every thing but wings
  Is my babe an angel!

Blue as heaven is are the eyes,
  'Neath the lids so waxen,
And the gold of morning lies
  In the ringlets flaxen.

Fragrant shrub, or tropic tree,
  Never yielded blossom
Half so lovely, sweet, as thee,
  Sleeping on my bosom !

When thy little dimpled cheek
  Mine is softly pressing,
Not a wish have I to seek
  Any other blessing.

Art thou, little baby, mine ?
  Earlier love effacing:
One whose smile is like to thine,
  Chides this long embracing.

No ! as drops of light and dew
  Glorify each other,
So shall we, life journey through
  Father, child, and mother.

## SEKO.

BRIGHT dames had kept the knight
  Long at the wassail;
Therefore his courser white
  Flew toward his castle.

Deep moaned the ocean flood,
  Howled the wind hoarser—
Right through the ringing wood
  Struck the gay courser.

Hoof-strokes had trod the flowers
  Where the rein slackened;
Fierce flames had left the towers
  Ruined and blackened.

One look of mute despair
  Gave he lost splendour;
One cry rose wildly there,
  Wildly, but tender.

Up from the dismal rocks
  Rose the sad echo—
Maid of the golden locks,
  Dewy-eyed Seko!

Once more with smothered pain
  Writhed his lip slightly,
Then 'neath a tightened rein
  Flew the steed lightly.

Hushed be thy stormy wrath,
  Desolate bosom;
Low in thy mountain path
  Lies the lost blossom.

Pale uncaressing lips
  Wait for the lover,
Pale as the plume that dips
  Softly above her.

Bright o'er the icy rocks
  Of the roused echo
Lay the long golden locks
  Of the dead Seko.

Drifting like silver rain
  Down o'er his master
Went the white courser's mane—
  Woful disaster!

## THE DESERTED FYLGIA.*

LIKE a meteor, radiant, streaming,
Seems her hair to me,
And thou bear'st her feet like lilies,
Dark and chilly sea!

Wannish fires enclasp her bosom,
Like the Northern Light,
And like icicles her fingers
Glisten, locked and white.

On the blue and icy ocean,
As a stony floor,
Toward thy boat, O dying Viking,
Walks she evermore!

Like a star on morning's forehead,
When the intense air,
Sweeping o'er the face of heaven,
Lays its far depths bare—

* "A Scandinavian warrior, having embraced Christianity, and being attacked by disease which he thought mortal, was naturally anxious that a spirit who had accompanied him through his pagan career should not attend him into that other world, where her society might involve him in disagreeable consequences. The persevering Fylgia, however, in the shape of a fair maiden, walked on the waves of the sea, after her Viking's ship."

Is the beauty of her smiling,
Pale and cold and clear—
What, O fearful, dying Viking,
Doth the maiden here?

Hath the wretched hell-maid, Belsta,
Ever crossed her way,
Weirdly driving herds of cattle,
Cattle dark and gray?

Hath she seen the maids of Skulda
Draw from Urda's well
Water where the awful snake-king
Gnaws the roots of hell?

Hath she seen the harts that ever
Haunt the ashen tree,
Keeping all its buds from blooming?
Viking, answer me!

Moaningly his white lips tremble,
But no voice replies—
Starlight in the blue waves frozen,
Seem his closing eyes.

Woman's lot is thine, O Fylgia,
Mourning broken faith,
And her mighty love outlasting
Chance and change and death!

# MUSIC.

There is music, deep and solemn,
Floating through the vaulted arch
When, in many an angry column,
Clouds take up their stormy march:
O'er the ocean billows, heaping
Mountains on the sloping sands,
There are ever wildly sweeping
Shapeless and invisible hands.

Echoes full of truth and feeling
From the olden bards sublime,
Are, like spirits, brightly stealing
Through the broken walls of time.
The universe, that glorious palace,
Thrills and trembles as they float,
Like the little blossom's chalice
With the humming of the mote.

On the air, as birds in meadows—
Sweet embodiments of song—
Leave their bright fantastic shadows
Trailing goldenly along.
Till, aside our armour laying,
We like prisoners depart,
In the soul is music playing
To the beating of the heart.

## ORPHAN'S SONG.

On the white cliffs of the ocean
  The sea-bird rests her wing:
For the meek and patient camel
  Of the desert, there's a spring:
But the shore hath rocks as steady
  Whereon weary feet may stand,
And fountains flow more sweetly
  From the meadow than the sand.

We are orphans, poor and homeless,
  And the tempest whistles loud;
But the stars of heaven are hiding
  In the meshes of the cloud.
With the sleet our locks are stiffened,
  And our path is white with snow,
And we leave the print of naked feet
  Behind us as we go.

But we've honest hearts, my brothers,
  And sinewy hands beside,
And our mother's benediction
  That she gave us when she died;
And whatever may befall us,
  We will never bow our souls
But to Him who kept the Hebrews
  In the furnace of hot coals.

## BRIDGES.

My friend, thou art mournful and heavy,
That life is a transient breath—
Disheartened, it may be, with hearing
The moan of the river of death.

Up! work out the fate of a hero,
Or perish at least in the strife;
Even we may be builders of bridges
For the passage of souls into Life.

As the wave of existence is drifting
And rushing to darkness and death,
Let us hew, with the sword of the spirit,
White blocks from the deep mine of faith.

The rainbow shall o'erarch our bridges,
Olives the pathway shall pave,
And the beautiful stone of the corner
Rest on the floor of the grave.

Like bright birds under the rafters
Shall hover the good deeds we do,
And the fair pillars shine with the beauty
Of lives to humanity true.

My friend, wilt thou lend me thy counsel?
And then, if thou wilt, we will strive
O'er the river of death to build bridges,
That souls may o'erpass it and live.

## BOOK OF LIGHT.

GENTLEST sister, I am weary—
Bring, oh, bring the Book of Light!
There are shadows dark and dreary
Settling on my heart to-night.

That alone can soothe my sadness,
That alone can dry my tears,
When I see no spot of gladness
Down the dusky vale of years.

Well I know that I inherit
All that sometimes makes me blest;
And in vain I ask my spirit
Why this feeling of unrest.

But all day have been around me
Voices that would not be still,
And the twilight shades have found me
Shrinking from a nameless ill.

Seeing not despair's swift lightning—
Hearing not the thunders roll,
Hands invisible are tightening
Bands of sorrow on my soul.

Out beneath the jewelled arches
Let us bivouac to-night,
And to soothe days' dusty marches
Bring, oh, bring the Book of Light!

## THE CHILD OF NATURE.

HASTE, haste, my gentle sisters,
 Break away from slumber's chain,
The light of morn streams redly
 Through my chamber lattice-pane !

I hear the wild birds calling
 With their sweet throats all in tune—
'Tis the goldenest of the mornings
 Of the merry month of June !

On the horizon's blue edges
 The sweet light dimly burns,
And the summer dew is dropping
 From the roses' crimson urns.

Leaving toilet and mirror—
 With the sunshine on the hill
I will let the breezes dally
 With my tresses as they will !

The spray-wreaths of the fountains
 In the light of such a morn,
Must be like the snowy fleeces
 Of the lambs among the corn.

Why should the heart be folded
 In the mantle of dim care,
In so glorious a temple
 For the offering up of prayer?

## WHERE REST THE DEAD?

ANSWER, thou star whose brightening ray
Foretells the gathering shades of night,
If so 'tis given thee, where are they
Who pass from mortal sight?

We know in some green isle of bliss,
Where clouds and tempests never roll,
There is a holier home than this—
A triumph for the soul!

The early birds, the summer flowers,
The tearful spring-time has restored;
But when shall they again be ours
O'er whom our love was poured?

We look to see the spirit's track,
And hear the stir of wings above,
And call, but win no answer back,
Nor token of their love.

While kindred smiles and tones of mirth
Are mingling brightly as the waves,
There still rests darkly on our hearth
A shadow from the graves.

Answer, thou star whose brightening ray
Foretells the gathering shades of night,
If so 'tis given thee, where are they
Who pass from mortal sight?

# POEMS BY PHŒBE CAREY.

# POEMS BY PHŒBE CAREY.

---

## A STORY.

WHILE silently our vessel glides,
  To-night, along the Adrian seas,
And while the lightly-heaving tides
  Are scarcely rippled by the breeze—
Thou, who, with cheek of beauty pale,
  Seem'st o'er some hidden grief to pine,
If thou wilt listen to a tale
  Of sorrow, it may lighten thine.
'Twas told me, sadly choked with tears;
  My eyes, it may be, too, were wet;
For, through the shadowy lapse of years,
  My memory keeps the record yet.
And he who told it long ago,
  Though scarcely passed his manhood's prime,
He seemed as one whose heart with wo
  Was seared and blighted ere its time.
And as he told his story o'er,
  Long vanished years came back to me;
For he had crossed my path before,
  Upon the land and on the sea.

When first by chance I saw his form,
  'Twas on the raging waves at night,
And if at all he saw the storm,
  He recked not of its angry might.
For while the dark and troubled skies
  Rung with accents of despair,
He never raised his tearful eyes,
  Nor lifted up his voice in prayer.
Once, thirsting for the cooling well,
  Beneath a fierce and burning sun,
And listening to the camel's bell,
  That music of the desert lone,
We reached a spot whose fountain made
  An Eden in that barren land;
And there, beneath the palm-tree's shade,
  We saw the lonely stranger stand.
And once, when twilight closed the flowers,
  I marked him on dark Jura's steep,
And twice amid thy sacred bowers,
  Gethsemane, I saw him weep.

But when I saw the mourner last,
  And heard the story of his woes,
'Twas where the solemn cypress cast
  Its shadow o'er man's last repose.
The sun had faded from the sky,
  With all his bright and glowing bars,
And solemn clouds were gliding by,
  In spectral silence o'er the stars.
And there, beside a grassy mound,
  In agony for words too deep,

And eyes bent sadly on the ground,
  I saw him clasp his hands and weep.
Though I had seen him on the sea
  Unmoved, when all beside were pale,
And weeping in Gethsemane,
  I never asked nor knew his tale.
But now, beside the tomb, at last,
  By kindly looks and words, I sought
To learn the story of the past,
  And win him from his troubled thought.
With lips all breathlessly apart,
  He listened to each soothing word;
The chord was touched within his heart,—
  The long untroubled fount was stirred.

"Companioned only by the dead,
  So many years I've lived alone,
I hardly thought," he sadly said,
  "To hear again a pitying tone.
But, stranger, friend, thy words are kind,
  And since thou fain wouldst learn my grief,
It may be that my heart will find,
  In utterance of its woes, relief.
Life's brightest scenes will I recall,
  And those where shade and sunshine blend,
And, if my lips can speak it all,
  I'll tell it even to the end.
My childhood! it were more than vain
  To tell thee that was glad as fleet;
While innocence and youth remain,
  Thou knowest that life's cup is sweet.

But when the soul of manhood beamed,
  In after years, upon my brow,—
(I know how darkly it is seamed
  With scars of guilt and sorrow now,)—
When, with the summer stars above,
  And dew-drops shining in the vale,
I told the story of my love
  To one who did not scorn the tale;
And when, in happiness and pride,
  Such as I never knew before,
I bore her to my home a bride,
  The measure of my bliss ran o'er.
Oh, in that bower of Eden blest,
  I fain would linger with my song;
It irks me so to tell the rest—
  The serpent did not spare it long.

"It was the eve of such a day
  As on creation dawned of old,
And all along the heavenly way
  The stars had set their lamps of gold.
That night I stood amid the throng
  Where banquet flowers were sweetly strown,
Where wine was poured with mirth and song,
  And where the smile of beauty shone.
When lost in pleasure's maze, and when
  My heart to reason's voice was steeled,
I tasted of the WINE-CUP, then—
  I tasted, and my doom was sealed!
That night the moments passed more fleet
  Than with my bride upon the hills;

That night I drank a draught more sweet
  Than water from the living rills.
It is a harder task to win
  The feet, at first, from right astray;
Yet if but once we yield to sin,
  How easy is the downward way!
Oh, if the spirit can be won
  In evil ways to enter in,
That first false step may lead us on
  Through all the labyrinths of sin:
And I resisted not the power
  That drew me first towards the bowl,
While firmer every day and hour
  The chains were fastened in my soul.
I saw hope's sunny fountain fail
  In her young heart who loved me so,
As day by day, her cheek grew pale
  With vigils and with tears of wo.

"Oh, if a kind and pitying word,
  If tones so sweet as thine have been,
My erring spirit could have heard,
  They might have saved me, even then.
But no; they named with scorn my name,
  And viewed me with reproachful eyes;
For all who saw my guilt and shame
  But looked upon me to despise.
And so I left my home and hearth,
  For haunts of wickedness and sin,
And sought, in wine and stronger mirth,
  To hush the voice of God within.

I have no record in my heart
Of how my days and weeks went by,
Save shadowy images that start
Like spectres still before mine eye.
As something indistinct and dim
Of sable hearse and funeral pall,
Of trailing robes and mournful hymn,
My memory keeps—and that is all!
But when, as from a horrid dream,
I woke, disturbed by nameless fears,
I sought beside the mountain stream
My home so dear in earlier years.
'Twas desolate—I called my bride,
And listened, but no answer came;
I made the hills and valleys wide
Re-echo vainly with her name!
And when I heard a step draw near,
And met a stranger's wondering gaze,
I asked, in tones of doubt and fear,
For that sweet friend of earlier days.
And then I followed where he led;
And as he left that singing stream,
I glided near him with a tread
Like guilty spirits in a dream:
He brought me to this quiet ground,
The last repose of wo and care,
And, pointing to that grassy mound,
He told me that MY BRIDE WAS THERE!

"I've been, for hopeless years since then,
A wanderer on the land and sea,

And little loved the homes of men,
  Or in their busy haunts to be;
And should not now have turned to tread
  This darkest scene of all my woes,
But something in my heart has said
  My life is hastening to its close.
And now I have no wish below,
  And no request for man to keep,
If thou, who know'st my tale of wo,
  Wilt lay me by my bride to sleep."

He paused, and, blinded by his tears,
  Bowed down with sorrow dark and deep,
The hoarded agony of years
  Broke forth, and then he ceased to weep:
But when he raised his eyes again,
  I saw, what was unseen till now,
That death, in characters too plain,
  Was written on that pallid brow.

Three little days; and then we laid
  That wreck of manhood and of pride
Beneath the gloomy cypress shade,
  To slumber with his stricken bride.

## THE LOVERS.

THOU marvellest why so oft her eyes
  Fill with the heavy dew of tears—
Have I not told thee that there lies
  A shadow darkly on her years?
Life was to her one sunny whole,
  Made up of visions fancy wove,
Till that the waters of her soul
  Were troubled by the touch of love.
I knew when first the sudden pause
  Upon her spirit's sunshine fell:
Alas! I little guessed the cause,
  'Twas hidden in her heart so well.
Our lives since early infancy
  Had flowed as rills together flow,
And now to hide her thought from me
  Was bitterer than to tell its wo.

One night, when clouds with anguish black
  A tempest in her bosom woke,
She crushed the bitter tear-drops back,
  And told me that her heart was broke!
I learned it when the autumn hours
  With wailing winds around us sighed—
'Twas summer when her love's young flowers
  Burst into glorious life and died:

No—now I can remember well,
'Twas the soft month of sun and shower;
A thousand times I've heard her tell
The season, and the very hour:
For now, whene'er the tear-drops start,
As if to ease its throbbing pain,
She leans her head upon my heart
And tells the very tale again.

'Tis something of a moon, that beamed
Upon her weak and trembling form,
And one beside, on whom she leaned,
That scarce had stronger heart or arm—
Of souls united there until
Death the last ties of life shall part,
And a fond kiss whose rapturous thrill
Still vibrates softly in her heart.

It is an era strange, yet sweet,
Which every woman's thought has known,
When first her young heart learns to beat
To the soft music of a tone;
That era when she first begins
To know what love alone can teach,
That there are hidden depths within
Which friendship never yet could reach:
And all earth has of bitter wo
Is light beside her hopeless doom
Who sees love's first sweet star below
Fade slowly till it sets in gloom.

There may be heavier grief to move
The heart that mourns an idol dead,
But one who weeps a living love
Has surely little left to dread.

I cannot tell why love so true
As theirs should only end in gloom;
Some mystery that I never knew
Was woven darkly with their doom.
I only know their dream was vain,
And that they woke to find it past,
And when by chance they met again,
It was not as they parted last.
His was not faith that lightly dies,
For truth and love as clearly shone
In the blue heaven of his soft eyes,
As the dark midnight of her own:
And therefore Heaven alone can tell
What are his living visions now;
But hers—the eye can read too well
The language written on her brow.

In the soft twilight, dim and sweet,
Once, watching by the lattice pane,
She listened for his coming feet,
For whom she never looked in vain:
Then hope shone brightly on her brow,
That had not learned its after fears—
Alas! she cannot sit there now,
But that her dark eyes fill with tears!

And every woodland pathway dim,
 And bower of roses cool and sweet,
That speak of vanished days and him,
 Are spots forbidden to her feet.
No thought within her bosom stirs,
 But wakes some feeling dark and dread:
God keep thee from a doom like hers—
 Of living when the hopes are dead!

---

## OUR HOMESTEAD.

Our old brown homestead reared its walls,
 From the wayside dust aloof,
Where the apple boughs could almost cast
 Their fruitage on its roof:
And the cherry-tree so near it grew,
 That when awake I've lain,
In the lonesome nights I've heard the limbs,
 As they creaked against the pane:
And those orchard trees, oh, those orchard trees!
 I've seen my little brothers rocked
In their tops by the summer breeze.

The sweet-brier under the window sill,
 Which the early birds made glad,
And the damask rose by the garden fence
 Were all the flowers we had.

I've looked at many a flower since then,
Exotics rich and rare,
That to other eyes were lovelier,
But not to me so fair;
For those roses bright, oh, those roses bright!
I have twined them with my sister's locks,
That are laid in the dust from sight!

We had a well, a deep old well,
Where the spring was never dry,
And the cool drops down from the mossy stones
Were falling constantly:
And there never was water half so sweet
As that in my little cup,
Drawn up to the curb by the rude old sweep,
Which my father's hand set up;
And that deep old well, oh, that deep old well!
I remember yet the plashing sound
Of the bucket as it fell.

Our homestead had an ample hearth,
Where at night we loved to meet;
There my mother's voice was always kind,
And her smile was always sweet;
And there I've sat on my father's knee,
And watched his thoughtful brow,
With my childish hand in his raven hair—
That hair is silver now!
But that broad hearth's light, oh, that broad hearth's light!
And my father's look, and my mother's smile,
They are in my heart to-night.

## THE FOLLOWERS OF CHRIST.

WHAT were thy teachings? Thou who hadst not where
In all this weary earth to lay thy head;
Thou who wert made the sins of men to bear,
And break with publicans thy daily bread!
Turning from Nazareth, the despised, aside,
And dwelling in the cities by the sea,
What were thy words to those who sat and dried
Their nets upon the rocks of Galilee?

Didst thou not teach thy followers here below,
Patience, long-suffering, charity, and love;
To be forgiving, and to anger slow,
And perfect, like our blessed Lord above?
And who were they, the called and chosen then,
Through all the world, teaching thy truth, to go?
Were they the rulers, and the chiefest men,
The teachers in the synagogue? Not so!
Makers of tents, and fishers by the sea,
These only left their all to follow thee.

And even of the twelve whom thou didst name
Apostles of thy holy word to be,
One was a devil; and the one who came
With loudest boasts of faith and constancy,

He was the first thy warning who forgot,
And said, with curses, that he knew thee not!
Yet were there some who in thy sorrows were
  To thee even as a brother and a friend,
And women, seeking out the sepulchre,
  Were true and faithful even to the end:
And some there were who kept the living faith
Through persecution even unto death.

But, Saviour, since that dark and awful day
  When the dread temple's vail was rent in twain,
And while the noontide brightness fled away,
  The gaping earth gave up her dead again;
Tracing the many generations down,
  Who have professed to love thy holy ways,
Through the long centuries of the world's renown,
  And through the terrors of her darker days—
Where are thy followers, and what deeds of love
Their deep devotion to thy precepts prove?

Turn to the time when o'er the green hills came
  Peter the Hermit from the cloister's gloom,
Telling his followers in the Saviour's name
  To arm and battle for the sacred tomb;
Not with the Christian armour—perfect faith,
  And love which purifies the soul from dross—
But holding in one hand the sword of death,
  And in the other lifting up the cross,
He roused the sleeping nations up to feel
All the blind ardour of unholy zeal!

With the bright banner of the cross unfurled,
And chanting sacred hymns, they marched, and yet
They made a pandemonium of the world,
More dark than that where fallen angels met:
The singing of their bugles could not drown
The bitter curses of the hunted down!
Richard, the lion-hearted, brave in war,
Tancred, and Godfrey, of the fearless band,
Though earthly fame had spread their names afar,
What were they but the scourges of the land?
And worse than these were men, whose touch would be
Pollution, vowed to lives of sanctity!

And in thy name did men in other days
Construct the Inquisition's gloomy cell,
And kindle persecution to a blaze,
Likest of all things to the fires of hell!
Ridley and Latimer—I hear their song
In calling up each martyr's glorious name,
And Cranmer, with the praises on his tongue
When his red hand dropped down amid the flame!
Merciful God! and have these things been done,
And in the name of thy most holy Son?

Turning from other lands grown old in crime,
To this, where Freedom's root is deeply set,
Surely no stain upon its folds sublime
Dims the escutcheon of our glory yet?

Hush! came there not a sound upon the air
Like captives moaning from their native shore—

Woman's deep wail of passionate despair
  For home and kindred seen on earth no more!
Yes, standing in the market-place, I see
  Our weaker brethren coldly bought and sold,
To be in hopeless, dull captivity,
  Driven forth to toil like cattle from the fold.
And hark! the lash, and the despairing cry
Of the strong man in perilous agony!

And near me I can hear the heavy sound
  Of the dull hammer borne upon the air:
Is a new city rising from the ground?
  What hath the artisan constructed there?
'Tis not a palace, nor an humble shed;
  'Tis not a holy temple reared by hands:
No!—lifting up its dark and bloody head
  Right in the face of Heaven, the scaffold stands;
And men, regardless of "Thou shalt not kill,"
  That plainest lesson in the Book of Light,
Even from the very altars tell us still
  That evil sanctioned by the law is right!
And preach in tones of eloquence sublime,
To teach mankind that murder is not crime!

And is there nothing to redeem mankind?
  No heart that keeps the love of God within?
Is the whole world degraded, weak, and blind,
  And darkened by the leprous scales of sin?
No, we will hope that some in meekness sweet,
Still sit, with trusting Mary, at thy feet.

For there are men of God, who faithful stand
  On the far ramparts of our Zion's wall,
Planting the cross of Jesus in some land
  That never listened to salvation's call.
And there are some, led by philanthropy,
  Men of the feeling heart and daring mind,
Who fain would set the hopeless captive free,
  And raise the weak and fallen of mankind.
And there are many in life's humblest way,
  Who tread like angels on a path of light,
Who warn the sinful when they go astray,
  And point the erring to the way of right;
And the meek beauty of such lives will teach
More than the eloquence of man can preach.

And, blessed Saviour! by thy life of trial,
  And by thy death, to free the world from sin,
And by the hope that man, though weak and vile,
  Hath something of divinity within—
Still will we trust, though sin and crime be met,
To see thy holy precepts triumph yet!

# SONNETS.

## I.

Down in the cold and noiseless wave of death,
Oh, pure and beautiful lost one that thou art,
Clasping the anchor of eternal faith
Closer and closer to thy trusting heart—
Didst thou fade from us, while our tearful eyes,
Here on the shore of sad mortality,
Gazed sorrowing on that form that ne'er shall rise
Till sounds the music of eternity.
Then shalt thou take the Saviour's hand in thine,
Not with his faith who held it falteringly,
But in the trustfulness of love divine,
And with him walk the waters of the sea;
Till, casting anchor, all thy toils shall cease
In the still haven of eternal peace.

## II.

The beautiful measure of thy trusting love
Survives the answering faith it knew of old;
Over the heart thy pleadings cannot move,
Slowly but sure the closing wave hath rolled:

The unpitying eyes thou meet'st burn not more bright,
  Though now thy lips with eloquent fervour speak,
And all thy passionate kisses may not light
  The crimson fires in the unchanging cheek.
How shall I give thee solace? Had she died,
  With love's sweet sunlight shining in her eyes,
Then might'st thou, casting selfish grief aside,
  Patiently wait reunion in the skies:
For better than the living faith estranged,
The love that goes down to the dead unchanged.

## III.

Look once again! yet mourn in holy trust,
  Near the still Presence softly, softly tread,
Before the dimness of the closing dust
  Soils the yet lingering beauty of the dead.
Look on the silent lip, whence oft hath flowed
  Such living truth as man hath seldom taught,
And the sereneness of that brow that glowed
  Earnest in life with pure and eloquent thought!
How silver-white has grown his reverend hair,
  Serving his Master in the way of truth:
For him, an age of active love and prayer
  Fulfilled the beautiful promise of his youth;
And what a triumph-hour is death to those
Faithful in life, yet happy in its close!

## IV.

LET me not feel thy pitying finger's grasp,
  Though dewy cool their pressure still may be,
Since they have learned to thrill within the clasp
  Of passionate love that trembled once for me!
Sweep back the beautiful tresses from thy brow,
  Nor let them, falling o'er me, blend with mine:
Dark as the glorious midnight in their flow,—
  My locks are paler in their fall than thine!
In thy deep eyes are lit the fires divine,
  That made the heart its early love forget;
So much they mock the softer light of mine
  I cannot calmly meet their glances yet;
Therefore, until this bitterness shall cease,
Leave me, that I may win my heart to peace!

## SYMPATHY.

In the same beaten channel still have run
The blessed streams of human sympathy;
And though I know this ever hath been done,
The why and wherefore I could never see:
Why some such sorrow for their griefs have won,
And some, unpitied, bear their misery,
Are mysteries, which thinking o'er and o'er
Has left me nothing wiser than before.

What bitter tears of agony have flowed
O'er the sad pages of some old romance!
How Beauty's cheek beneath those drops has glowed,
That dimmed the sparkling lustre of her glance,
And on some love-sick maiden is bestowed,
Or some rejected, hapless knight, perchance,
All her deep sympathies, until her moans
Stifle the nearer sound of living groans!

Oh, the deep sorrow for their sufferings felt,
Where is found something "better days" to prove!
What heart above their downfall will not melt,
Who in a "higher circle" once could move!
For such, mankind have ever freely dealt
Out the full measure of their pitying love,
Because they witnessed, in their wretchedness,
Their friends grow fewer, and their fortunes less.

But for some humble peasant girl's distress,
Some real being left to stem the tide,
Who saw her young heart's wealth of tenderness
Betrayed, and trampled on, and flung aside—
Who seeks her out, to make her sorrows less?
What noble lady o'er her tale hath cried?
None! for the records of such humble grief
Obtain not human pity—scarce belief.

And as for their distress, who from the first
Have had no fortune and no friends to fail—
Those who in poverty were born and nursed—
For such, by men, are placed without the pale
Of sympathy,—since they are deemed the worst
Who are the humblest, and if Want assail
And bring them harder toil, 'tis only said,
"They have been used to labour for their bread!"

Oh, the unknown, unpitied thousands found
Huddled together, hid from human sight
By fell disease or gnawing famine, bound
To some dim, crowded garret, day and night,
Or in unwholesome cellars underground,
With scarce a breath of air, or ray of light!
Hunger, and rags, and labour ill repaid—
These are the things that ask our tears and aid.

And these ought not to be; it is not well
Here in this land of Christian liberty,
That honest worth in hopeless want should dwell,
Unaided by our care and sympathy;

And is it not a burning shame to tell
 We have no means to check such misery,
When wealth from out our treasury freely flows,
To wage a deadly warfare with our foes!

It is all wrong; yet men begin to deem
 The days of darkest gloom are nearly done;
A something, like the first bright golden beam
 That heralds in the coming of the dawn,
Breaks on the sight. Oh, if it be no dream,
 How shall we haste that blessed era on!
For there is need that on men's hearts should fall
A spirit that shall sympathize with all.

---

## MEMORIES.

"She loved me, but she left me."

Memories on memories! to my soul again
 There come such dreams of vanished love and bliss,
That my wrung heart, though long inured to pain,
 Sinks with the fulness of its wretchedness.
Thou dearer far than all the world beside!
 Thou who didst listen to my love's first vow!
Once I had fondly hoped to call thee bride—
 Is the dream over? comes the awakening now?
And is this hour of wretchedness and tears
The only guerdon for my wasted years?

And did I love thee; when by stealth we met
  In the sweet evenings of that summer-time,
Whose pleasant memory lingers with me yet,
  As the remembrance of a better clime
Might haunt a fallen angel. And oh! thou,
  Thou who didst turn away and seek to bind
Thy heart from breaking, thou hast felt ere now
  A heart like thine o'ermastereth the mind;
Affection's power is stronger than thy will;
Ah! thou didst love me, and thou lovest me still.

My heart could never yet be taught to move
  With the calm even pulses that it should,
Turning away from those that it should love,
  And loving whom it should not; it hath wooed
Beauty forbidden—I may not forget—
  And thou, oh! thou canst never cease to feel;
But time, which hath not changed affection, yet
  Hath taught at least one lesson—to conceal;
So none, but thou, who see my smiles shall know
The silent bleeding of the heart below.

## MORALIZINGS.

HARK to the triumph for a victory won,
   Shaking the solid earth whereon we stand!
What noble action hath the Nation done,
   That thus rejoicing echoes through the land?
Hath she beheld life's inequality—
   How, still, her stronger sons the weak oppress,
And, in the spirit of philanthropy,
   Made the deep sum of human anguish less?
Or hath she risen up, at last, to free
The hopeless slave from his captivity?

No, not for these the shout is heard to-night
   Waking its echoes in each vale and glen,
Not that the precepts of the Lord of Light
   Have found a dwelling in the hearts of men;
'Tis that a battle hath been fought and won,
   That the deep cannon's note is heard afar,
Telling us of the bloody conflict done,
   That Victory hovers o'er our ranks in war,
And that her soldiery their triumph sing
In the broad shadow of her starry wing.

And war is here! Impatient for the fight,
   Our Nation in her majesty arose,
Even as the restless lion in his might
   Up from the swelling of the Jordan goes,

And, with a trampling noise that shook each hill,
  On to the conflict madly hath she rushed,
Vowing to falter not, nor yield, until
  The life from out a Nation's heart is crushed;
Until her hapless sons are made to feel
The bloody vengeance of her iron heel!

And what will be our gain, though we return
  Proudly victorious from each battle plain?
A weakened Nation will be left to mourn
  Her bravest heroes in the conflict slain;
Her treasury drained; our broad and goodly land
  Filled with the orphan and the widowed wife;
A soldiery corrupted to disband,
  Unfit for useful toil or virtuous life;
And a long train of evils yet to be
Darkly entailed upon posterity!

And this is glory! This is what hath been
  To ages back the proudest theme of song,
And, dazzled by its glare, man has not seen
  Beneath its pageantry the deadly wrong.
Deeming it fame to tread where heroes trod,
  In his career he has not paused, or known
That all are children of the selfsame God,
  And that our brother's interest is our own;
For man that hardest lesson has to learn,
Still to forgive, and good for ill return.

But oh! for all will come that solemn hour
  When memory calls to mind each deed of sin,

And the world's hollow praise can have no power
 To still the voice of conscious guilt within.
And grant, O Lord of Love, that it may be
 My lot, when on the brink of death I press,
To think of some slight act of charity,
 Some pang of human wretchedness made less,
So, that in numbering o'er life's deeds again,
I then may deem I have not lived in vain!

---

## DREAMING OF HEAVEN.

I SIT where the shadows of twilight steal o'er me,
 While the wild birds are warbling their last fitful hymn,
And I think of the loved who have entered before me
 That dwelling whose glory shall never grow dim.

For ever the land of the spirits seems nearer,
 When twilight steals over the earth's quiet breast,
And the harps of the angels sound sweeter and clearer,
 What time the last day-beams go out in the west.

Oh! if all my dreams were as bright and elysian
 As those which the eve to my spirit still brings,
I could sit here for ever to woo the sweet vision,
 And dream about heaven and heavenly things!

For I long to be up where the seraphim gather
 With the ransomed of Zion whom Jesus has blest,
And where, in the smile of our heavenly Father,
 Our purified spirits for ever shall rest!

## MORNING THOUGHTS.

CROSSING the east with gold and crimson bars,
  Comes the imperial King of day and light,
And, shaken by his tread, the burning stars
  Drop from the regal diadem of night.
Surely the dawn was not more fair than this
  When Eden's roses in fresh beauty burst,
And morning, blushing at her loveliness,
  Looked down upon the young creation first:
When all below was innocent, and when
The angels walked in Paradise with man.

How equally the gifts of God come down
  To all the creatures which his hand has made;
The beams that wake the children of renown,
  Fall softly on the peasant in the glade.
The dawn that calls the eagle up to fly
  From her proud eyrie to the mountain's height,
Visits the lowly lark as smilingly,
  When from the vale she takes her homeward flight:
Morning and life and sunshine, these are things
That are not meant to be the wealth of kings!

Freedom at least from homeless poverty,
  A soul unbowed by fetters or by pain,
One heart whose faith has still been true to me,
  These things are mine, and why should I complain?

Complain! when God has been so good to me,
  And when his blessings with my days increase,
Giving for every day of misery
  A recompense of tranquil days of peace:
Even as the morning with her smiles and light
Is over-payment for the weary night.

---

## RESOLVES.

I HAVE said I would not meet him; have I said the words in vain?
Sunset burns along the hill-tops, and I'm waiting here again.
But my promise is not broken, though I stand where once we met;
When I hear his coming footsteps, I can fly him even yet.

We have stood here oft when evening deepened slowly o'er the plain,
But I must not, dare not, meet him in the shadows here again;
For I could not turn away and leave that pleading look and tone,
And the sorrow of his parting would be bitter as my own.

In the dim and distant ether the first star is shining through,
And another and another tremble softly in the blue:

Should I linger but one moment in the shadows where
I stand,
I shall see the vine-leaves parted, with a quick impatient
hand.

But I will not wait his coming! he will surely come
once more;
Though I said I would not meet him, I have told him
so before;
And he knows the stars of evening see me standing here
again—
Oh, he surely will not leave me now to watch and wait
in vain!

'Tis the hour, the time of meeting! in one moment
'twill be past;
And last night he stood beside me; was that blessed
time the last?
I could better bear my sorrow, could I live that parting
o'er;
Oh, I wish I had not told him that I would not come
*once* more!

Could that have been the night-wind moved the branches
thus apart?
Did I hear a coming footstep, or the beating of my
heart?
No! I hear him, I can see him, and my weak resolves
are vain;
I will fly, but to his bosom, and to leave it not again!

## THE MARINER'S BRIDE.

O'ER the dark waters now my bounding bark
May bear me onward wheresoe'er it will:
I care not though the angry sky be dark,
Light of my being! thou art with me still.
Yes, let the heaving billows lash the deck,
And the red lightning tremble on the sea;
So that thy faithful arms are round my neck,
My heart will never tremble;—for with thee
I know my soul within would still be brave
If every gaping billow showed a grave.

Once I had feared the raging of the sea,
When the wild tempest in its fury burst;
But, bride of beauty! standing thus with thee,
The angry elements may do their worst.
And should our vessel founder on a rock,
Or cast us on some desert shore to die,
Unshrinkingly my soul will meet the shock,
If thou with that inspiring brow art nigh:
For, folding thee, my gentle bride, to sleep,
Closer, and closer, to this fainting breast,
We should go down as calmly to the deep
As a young infant to its cradle-rest.
And though the water-wraith should stir the sea,
And the wild tempest move the waves above,

Securely peaceful would my slumber be
With thee, my stricken bride of youth and love;
For thou wouldst cheer the darkness of the grave,
As the bright sea-star lights the ocean cave!

---

## THE PRISONER'S LAST NIGHT.

THE last red gold had melted from the sky,
Where the sweet sunset lingered soft and warm,
A starry night was gathering silently
The jewelled mantle round her regal form;
While the invisible fingers of the breeze
Shook the young blossoms lightly from the trees.

Yet were there breaking hearts beneath the stars,
Though the hushed earth lay smiling in the light,
And the dull fetters and the prison bars
Saw bitter tears of agony that night,
And heard such burning words of love and truth
As wring the life-drops from the heart of youth.

For he, whom men relentless doomed to die,
Parted with one who loved him till the last;
With many a vow of faith and constancy
The long, long watches of the night were passed;
Till, heavily and slow, the prison door
Swung back, and told them that their hour was o'er.

'Twas his last night on earth! and God alone
  Can tell the anguish of that stricken one,
Fettered in darkness to the dungeon stone,
  And doomed to perish with the rising sun;
And she, whose faith through all was vainly true,
Her heart was broken—and she perished too!

And will this win an erring brother back
  To the sweet paths of pleasantness and peace?
"While crimes are punished but by crime more black,"
  Will sin, and wickedness, and sorrow cease?
No! crime will never cease to scourge the land,
So long as blood is on her ruler's hand!

And oh! how long will hearts in sin and pride
  Reject His blessed precepts, who of yore
Taught men forgiveness on the mountain side,
  And spoke of love and mercy by the shore?
How long will power, with such despotic sway,
Trample unfriended weakness in its way?

Hasten, O Lord of Light, that glorious time,
  When man no more shall spurn thy wise command,
Filling the earth with wretchedness and crime,
  And making guilt a plague-spot on the land;
Hasten the time, that blood no more shall cry
Unceasingly for vengeance to the sky!

## SONG OF THE HEART.

THEY may tell for ever of worlds of bloom
Beyond the skies and beyond the tomb;
Of the sweet repose, and the rapture there,
That are not found in a world of care;
But not to me can the present seem
Like a foolish tale or an idle dream.

Oh, I know that the bowers of heaven are fair,
And I know that the waters of life are there;
But I do not long for their happy flow,
While there bursts such fountains of bliss below;
And I would not leave, for the rest above,
The faithful bosom of trusting love!

There are angels here; they are seen the while
In each love-lit brow and each gentle smile;
There are seraph voices, that meet the ear
In the kindly tone and the word of cheer;
And light, such light as they have above,
Beams on us here, from the eyes of love.

Yet, when it cometh my time to die,
I would turn from this bright world willingly;
Though, even then, would the thoughts of this
Tinge every dream of that land of bliss;

And I fain would lean on the loved for aid,
Nor walk alone through the vale and shade.

And if 'tis mine, till life's changes end,
To keep the heart of one faithful friend,
Whatever the trials of earth may be,—
On the peaceful shore, or the restless sea,
In a palace home, or the wilderness,—
There is heaven for me in a world like this!

---

## MAN BELIEVES THE STRONG.

Oh! in this world, where all is fair and bright,
  Save human wickedness and human pride,
Marring what else were lovely to the sight,
  It is a truth that may not be denied,
However deeply we deplore the wrong,
Man hath believed, and still believes the strong.

When injured and defenceless woman stands,
  Haply the child of innocence or youth,
And lifts to heaven her pleading voice and hands
  In all the moving eloquence of truth,
Who will believe, in that most trying hour,
Her words who is not strong in wealth or power?

Or let the slave, of all on earth bereft,
  Stand up to plead before a human bar;
And though the fetters and the lash have left
  Upon his limbs the deep-attesting scar,
Who trusts his tale, or who will rise to save
From wrong and injury the outcast slave?

If a poor, friendless criminal appear,—
  A criminal which men themselves have made,
By the injustice and oppression here,—
  Who to pronounce him "*guilty*" is afraid?
But who, if rank or wealth were doomed thereby,
Would speak that final word as fearlessly?

Oh, where so much of wrong and sorrow are,
  There must be need of an unfaltering trust
In His all-seeing watchfulness and care,
  Whose ways to man below we know are just;
In Him, whose love has numbered every tear
Wrung from his weak, defenceless creatures here.

And there is need of earnest, full belief,
  And patient work, to bring that holier day
When there shall be redress for humblest grief,
  And equal right and justice shall have sway;
And we will strive, in trustfulness sublime,
Hoping our eyes may see the blessed time!

## THE CHRISTIAN WOMAN.

OH! beautiful as morning in those hours
When, as her pathway lies along the hills,
Her golden fingers wake the dewy flowers,
And softly touch the waters of the rills,
Was she who walked more faintly day by day,
Till silently she perished by the way.

It was not hers to know that perfect heaven
Of passionate love returned by love as deep,
Not hers to sing the cradle-song at even,
Watching the beauty of her babe asleep;
"Mother and brethren"—these she had not known,
Save such as do the Father's will alone.

Yet found she something still for which to live—
Hearths desolate, where angel-like she came;
And "little ones," to whom her hand could give
A cup of water in her Master's name;
And breaking hearts, to bind away from death
With the soft hand of pitying love and faith.

She never won the voice of popular praise,
But, counting earthly triumph as but dross,
Seeking to keep her Saviour's perfect ways,
Bearing in the still path his blessed cross,

She made her life, while with us here she trod,
A consecration to the will of God.

And she hath lived and laboured not in vain—
Through the deep prison-cells her accents thrill,
And the sad slave leans idly on his chain,
And hears the music of her singing still;
While little children, with their innocent praise,
Keep freshly in men's hearts her Christian ways.

And what a beautiful lesson she made known—
The whiteness of her soul sin could not dim;
Ready to lay down on God's altar-stone
The dearest treasure of her life for Him,
Her flame of sacrifice never, never waned;
How could she live and die so self-sustained?

For friends supported not her parting soul,
And whispered words of comfort, kind and sweet,
When treading onward to that final goal,
Where the still Bridegroom waited for her feet;
Alone she walked, yet with a fearless tread,
Down to Death's chamber and his bridal bed!

## THE HOMESICK PEASANT.

OH! I am sick of cities; all night long
  Orchards and corn-fields waved before my sight,
Till the quick moving of the restless throng
  Broke on that pleasant vision of the night
With an unwelcome sound, and called my feet
Back from the meadows to the crowded street.

I grew a child of Nature on the hills,
  Learning no lessons from the lips of Art,
And the restraint of cities cramps and chills
  The warm, impulsive feelings of my heart;
Even the ceaseless stir and motion here
Grates with a jarring sound upon my ear.

It is not like my childhood: from the trees,
  And from the flowers that grew beneath my feet,
And from the artless whispers of the breeze,
  I never learned the lessons of deceit;
They never taught me that my heart should hide
Its thoughts and feelings with a mask of pride.

And therefore with the morning I awake,
  To feel a homesick yearning for the hills—
A thirst no water on the earth can slake,
  Save the clear gushing of my native rills;

And I once more upon their banks would stand,
Free as the breezes of my native land.

Give me a sweet home, set among the trees,
With friends whose words are ever kind and true,
And books whose stories should instruct and please,
When round the quiet hearth the household drew;
For in their pleasant pages I can find
All I would learn of cities and mankind.

---

## HOMES FOR ALL.

Columbia, fairest nation of the world,
Sitting in queenly beauty in the west,
With all thy banners round about thee furled,
Nursing the cherub Peace upon thy breast;
Never did daughter of a kingly line
Look on a lovelier heritage than thine!

Thou hast deep forests stretching far away,
The giant growth of the long centuries,
From whose dim shadows to the light of day
Come forth the mighty rivers toward the seas,
To walk like happy lovers, hand in hand,
Down through the green vales of our pleasant land.

Thou hast broad prairies, where the lovely flowers
Blossom and perish with the changing year;

Where harvests wave not through the summer hours,
 Nor with the autumn ripen in the ear;
And beautiful lakes that toss their milky spray
Where the strong ship hath never cleaved its way.

And yet with all thy broad and fertile land,
 Where hands sow not, nor gather in the grain,
Thy children come and round about thee stand,
 Asking the blessing of a home in vain,—
Still lingering, but with feet that long to press
Through the green windings of the wilderness.

In populous cities do men live and die,
 That never breathe the pure and liberal air;
Down where the damp and desolate rice-swamps lie,
 Wearying the ear of Heaven with constant prayer,
Are souls that never yet have learned to raise
Under God's equal sky the psalm of praise.

Turn not, Columbia! from their pleading eyes;
 Give to thy sons that ask of thee a home;
So shall they gather round thee, not with sighs,
 But as young children to their mother come;
And brightly to the centuries shall go down
The glory that thou wearest like a crown.

## HARVEST GATHERING.

THE last days of the summer: bright and clear
Shines the warm sun down on the quiet land,
Where corn-fields, thick and heavy in the ear,
Are slowly ripening for the labourer's hand;
Seed-time and harvest—since the bow was set,
Not vainly has man hoped your coming yet!

To the quick rush of sickles, joyously
The reapers in the yellow wheat-fields sung,
And bound the pale sheaves of the ripened rye,
When the first tassels of the maize were hung;
That precious seed into the furrow cast
Earliest in spring-time, crowns the harvest last.

Ever, when summer's sun burns faint and dim,
And rare and few the pleasant days are given,
When the sweet praise of our thanksgiving hymn
Makes beautiful music in the ear of Heaven,
I think of other harvests whence the sound
Of singing comes not as the sheaves are bound.

Not where the rice-fields whiten in the sun,
And the warm South casts down her yellow fruit,
Shout they the labours of the autumn done—
For there Oppression casts her deadly root,

And they, who sow and gather in that clime,
Share not the treasures of the harvest-time.

God of the seasons! thou who didst ordain
   Bread for the eater who shall plant the soil,
How have they heard thee, who have forged the chain
   And built the dungeon for the sons of toil?
Burdening their hearts, not with the voice of prayer,
But the dull cries of almost dumb despair.

They who would see that growth of wickedness
   Planted where now the peaceful prairie waves,
And make the green paths of our wilderness
   Red with the torn and bleeding feet of slaves—
Forbid it, Heaven! and let the sharp axe be
Laid at the root of that most poison tree!

Let us behold its deadly leaves begin
   A fainter shadow o'er the world to cast,
And the long day that nursed its growth of sin
   Wane to a sunset that shall be its last;
So that the day-star, rising from the sea,
Shall light a land whose children will be free!

## LIFE IS NOT VANITY.

ARE ye not erring teachers
Who tell us, that below
There is no sparkling fountain
Where living waters flow;
That all earth's well-springs bubble up
With bitter drops of wo?

That life's a night of darkness,
With scarce a cheering star,—
That we cannot make our trials
Less bitter than they are,—
That we should think of heaven alone,
And heaven itself is far.

No marvel earth is dark to you
Who thus in shadows keep,—
That you cannot see the day-spring
When you close your eyes and sleep;
Or that earth is but a vale of tears
For you who sit and weep.

You tell us of the happiness
Of the unchanging sphere,
Because the loved and loving there
To bless us will be near;

If that be heaven, what hinders us
  To make a heaven here?

Oh, would we rouse from slumber,
  Life hath something to be done;
We may lose the prize by faltering,
  Which exertion might have won;
And when we strive to help ourselves,
  The Lord will aid us on.

And if we be immortal,
  As we believe and know,
Then is the life eternal
  Begun in life below;
And hath it been ordained by heaven,
  That it should be in wo?

No! and though trailing shadows
  O'er our pathway sometimes move,
Yet below, as in the life to come,
  All things are ruled in love,
And God will bless as willingly
  As he will do above!

And if we cheer life's marches,
  And smooth the path beneath,
If we labour for advancement
  With a true and earnest faith;
We shall stand prepared for lengthened years,
  Or for the call of death!

## PRAYER.

Father! thou didst hear my prayer:
When I plead with thee to spare,
When I asked for length of years,
Thou didst pitying see my tears,
And thy words in answer were,
"Respite from the sepulchre!"

Lo! no more the prayer I raise:
Life hath waned to evil days;
Veiling in the dust my woes,
I would bless the grave's repose;
Sweeter, sweeter would it be,
Than a lover's dream to me.

Long enough thy child hath been
Struggling in a world of sin,
Long enough have doubts assailed,
Long enough the flesh prevailed,
Long enough hath sorrow tried
One it hath not purified.

In life's hours of rosy dawn,
Hope with white hand led me on,
Showing gorgeous imagery
Of a happier time to be;
But, in noonday's clearer flame,
Blest fruition never came.

Hastening now towards its close
Is the day that brightly rose,
And the hope that fled its prime
Comes not at the evening time;
Hear me, pity, and recall,
Ere the midnight shadows fall!

Willing, eager to depart,
Old in years and old in heart,
Waiting but the messenger
To unseal the sepulchre,
Lo! again to Thee I come—
Take me, Father, take me home!

---

## MORNING.

Sadly, when the day was done,
To his setting waned the sun;
Heavily the shadows fell,
And the wind, with fitful swell,
Echoed through the forest dim
Like a friar's ghostly hymn.

Mournful on the wall, afar,
Walked the evening sentry-star;
Burning clear, and cold, and lone,
Midnight's constellations shone;

While the hours, with solemn tread,
Passed like watchers by the dead.

Now at last the Morning wakes,
And the spell of darkness breaks,
On the mountains, dewy sweet,
Standing with her rosy feet,
While her golden fingers fair
Part the soft flow of her hair.

With the dew from flower and leaf
Flies the heavy dew of grief;
From the darkness of my thought,
Night her solemn aspect caught;
And the morning's joys begin,
As a morning breaks within.

God's free sunshine on the hills,
Soft mists hanging o'er the rills,
Blushing flowers of loveliness
Trembling with the light wind's kiss—
Oh! the soul forgets its care,
Looking on a world so fair!

Morning wooes me with her charms,
Like a lover's pleading arms;
Soft above me bend her skies,
As a lover's tender eyes;
And my heavy heart of pain,
Trembling, thrills with hope again.

## BURIAL HYMN.

EARTH to earth, and dust to dust!
Here, in calm and holy trust,
We have made her quiet bed
With the pale hosts of the dead,
And, with hearts that, stricken, weep,
Come to lay her down to sleep.

From life's weary cares set free,
Mother Earth, she comes to thee!
Hiding from its ills and storms
In the shelter of thine arms:
Peaceful, peaceful be her rest,
Here upon thy faithful breast.

And when sweetly from the dust
Heaven's last summons calls the just,
Saviour! when the nations rise
Up to meet thee in the skies,
Gently, gently, by the hand,
Lead her to the better land!

## SONG OF THE REFORMED.

Seeking its place of rest,
Each in its quiet nest,
All the glad warblers have hushed their last song;
And the first star of night,
With her faint silver light,
Guideth my homeward steps safely along.

Oh! to that quiet home,
With what delight I come,
When from the cares of the day I am free;
For with her happy smile,
There my young wife the while
Sits by the lattice pane watching for me.

But when I sought the board
Where the red wine is poured,
Oft has she fled when my footsteps drew near,
And nestling down to rest,
Close to that faithful breast,
Has my young infant turned from me in fear.

Silently then each day
Passed her sad life away—
Silently then was our sweet child caressed;

Now our low cabin rings
With the glad song she sings,
Rocking it nightly to sleep on her breast.

There I can see the light
Where our warm hearth is bright,
Oh! is there bliss more ecstatic above
Than this full heart can know,
Blest with your smiles below,
Wife of my bosom and child of my love?

---

## THE COLD WATER ARMY.

Firmly they still have stood,
A true and fearless band,
For the noble cause of human good
Hath nerved each heart and hand.
And they fear not the frowns of earth,
The mocking sneers of men,
For they fight for the sacred home and hearth,
For their trampled rights again.

In their ranks, no longer thin and weak,
Are men of every age,
From the stripling slight, with a beardless cheek,
To the silver-headed sage.
Oh, their hosts would darken the summer sea,
Were their banners all outspread,

And the dens of guilt rock tremblingly
  With their firm and heavy tread.

They come not, an invading band,
  With dreams of high renown,
To spoil the homes of our happy land,
  And trample her vineyards down;
But to hunt that monster of sin and crime,
  Which the slaves of the wine-cup know,
Who tracks his way in a path of slime
  O'er the fairest flowers below.

For undisturbed has he roamed the earth
  Till his serpent brood have come
To nest themselves in the very hearth
  Of many a once bright home.
Yet, hearing the widow and orphan's sigh,
  And knowing he wounds to kill,
There are those so deaf to a nation's cry
  They would shield the monster still.

But our army follows with noiseless tread
  Wherever he winds his way,
As, feeling the bruise on his venomed head,
  He shrinks from the light of day;
And ne'er on the unsheathed sword and spear
  Will their hand relax its grasp,
Till they pause, and lean on their arms, to hear
  The sound of his dying gasp.

## COMING HOME.

How long it seems since first we heard
  The cry of "Land in sight!"
Our vessel surely never sailed
  So slowly till to-night.
When we discerned the distant hills,
  The sun was scarcely set,
And now the noon of night is passed,
  They seem no nearer yet.

Where the blue Rhine reflected back
  Each frowning castle wall,
Where, in the forest of the Hartz,
  Eternal shadows fall—
Or where the yellow Tiber flowed
  By the old hills of Rome,
I never felt such restlessness,
  Such longing for our home.

Dost thou remember, oh! my friend,
  When we beheld it last,
How shadows from the setting sun
  Upon our cot were cast?
Three summer-times upon its walls
  Have shone for us in vain;
But, oh! we're hastening homeward now,
  To leave it not again.

There, as the last star dropped away
  From Night's imperial brow,
Did not our vessel "round the point?"
  The land looks nearer now!
Yes, as the first faint beams of day
  Fall on our native shore,
They're dropping anchor in the bay—
  We're home, we're home once more!

---

## THE REEFER.

Yes, sailor, when the angry deep
  Its war with heaven is waging,
I'll tell thee why I sit and weep
  When thus the storm is raging.
Once when the sea, as now, was tossed
  With fierce and wild commotion,
I stood unheeding on the coast,
  And watched the troubled ocean.

For as the arrowy bolts were hurled
  In fiery wrath from heaven,
We saw afar, with canvas furled,
  A ship through darkness driven.
I had a brother then, whose bark
  Upon the sea was riding,
And when I saw that vessel dark,
  I knew his hand was guiding.

And now, as fiercer came the light,
  And as the storm grew drearer,
We saw her through the gathering night
  Come near the strand, and nearer!
Already fancy clasped once more
  The form so fondly cherished,
When, reaching to the fatal shore,
  That vessel struck and perished!

And now, upon the sea, whene'er
  The black clouds o'er us hover,
I see that frail bark strike, and hear
  The shriek that rose above her!
No change can lull my thoughts to sleep,
  No time my grief assuages;
And therefore, sailor, do I weep,
  When thus the tempest rages.

---

## A TIME TO DIE.

LIKE the music deep and solemn
    In some ruined church,
Floating over crumbling column
    And fallen arch;
Through the naked branches trailing
    Low on the ground,
Come the winds of autumn wailing
    With a ghostly sound.

Over all below a feeling
Of quiet reigns,
Like a drowsy numbness stealing
Through the veins.
Even the sun, in the dim haze mourning,
Hides his head,
Like a sickly taper burning
Beside the dead.

And all day one feeling busy
In my soul hath wrought,
Till heart and brain are dizzy
With the solemn thought.
In the shadow of deep dejection
I sit and sigh,
With but one sad reflection,
"A TIME TO DIE!"

O God of the soul immortal!
If death be near,
Teach me to tread that portal
And not to fear.
Keep thou my feet from turning
Aside to die;
Let my lamp be filled and burning
For the "MIDNIGHT CRY!"

## DEATH SCENE.

DYING, still slowly dying,
As the hours of night wore by,
She had lain since the light of sunset
Was red on the evening sky.

Till after the middle watches,
As we softly near her trod,
When her soul from its prison fetters
Was loosed by the hand of God.

One moment her pale lips trembled
With the triumph she might not tell,
As the light of the life immortal
On her spirit's vision fell.

Then the look of rapture faded,
And the beautiful smile waxed faint,
As that in some convent picture
On the face of a dying saint.

And we felt in the lonesome midnight,
As we sat by the silent dead,
What a light on the path going downward
The steps of the righteous shed :

When we thought how with feet unshrinking
She came to the Jordan's tide,
And, taking the hand of the Saviour,
Went up on the heavenly side !

## THE PLACE OF GRAVES.

How often, in the summers gone,
I've stood where these memorials rise,
And every time the spot had grown
Less and less lonely to mine eyes.

The first I ever loved that died
Sleeps here, where these sweet roses wave;
A maiden, with life's paths untried,
She left the sunshine for the grave.

And what a place of desolate gloom
Seemed then to me the realm of death,
Though she I loved went calmly down,
In all the trustfulness of faith.

The next, a sweet lamb of the fold,
An infant, lulled to slumber lay,
With her pale locks of finest gold
Put softly from her brow away.

But when the patient mother prest
To her meek lips the bitter cup,
And came with those she loved to rest,
Till God shall call the sleepers up,

Then the dim pathway grew more clear,
That leads through darkness to the light,
And death has never seemed so drear,
Nor heaven so distant from my sight.

## PARTING AND MEETING.

On the casement, closed and lonesome,
Is falling the autumn rain,
And my heart to-night is heavy
With a sense of unquiet pain.

Not that the leaves are dying
In the kiss of the traitor frost,
And not that the summer flowers
On the bitter winds are tossed.

And not that the reaper's singing
The time no longer cheers,
Bringing home through the mellow starlight
The sheaves and the yellow ears.

No, not from these am I sighing,
As the hours pass slow and dull,
For God in his own time maketh
All seasons beautiful.

But one of our household number
Sits not by the hearth-fire's light,
And right on her pathway beating
Is the rain of this autumn night.

And therefore my heart is heavy
  With a sense of unquiet pain,
For, but Heaven can tell if the parted
  Shall meet in the earth again.

But knowing God's love extendeth
  Wherever his children are,
And tenderly round about them
  Are the arms of his watchful care;

With him be the time and the season
  Of our meeting again with thee,
Whether here on these earthly borders,
  Or the shore of the world to be.

---

## DEATH OF A FRIEND.

Where leaves by bitter winds are heaped
  In the deep hollows, damp and cold,
And the light snow-shower, silently,
  Is falling on the yellow mould,

Sleeps one who was our friend below—
  With meek hands folded on her breast,
When the first flowers of summer died,
  We softly laid her down to rest.

By her were blessings freely strewn,
As roses by the summer's breath;
Yet nothing in her perfect life
Was half so lovely as her death.

In the meek beauty of a faith
Which few have ever proved like her,
She shrunk not even when she felt
The chill breath of the sepulchre.

Heavier, and heavier still, she leaned
Upon His arm who died to save,
As step by step he led her down
To the still chamber of the grave.

'Twas at the midnight's solemn watch
She sunk to slumber, calm and deep—
The golden fingers of the dawn
Shall never wake her from that sleep.

From him, who was her friend below,
She turned to meet her Heavenly Guide;
And the sweet children of her love,
She left them sleeping when she died.

Her last of suns went calmly down,
And when the morn rose bright and clear,
Hers was a holier Sabbath-day
Than that which dawned upon us here.

## LOVE AT THE GRAVE.

REMEMBRANCER of nature's prime,
And herald of her fading near,
The last month of the summer time
Of leaves and flowers is with us here.

More eloquent than lip can preach
To every heart that hopes and fears,
What solemn lessons does it teach
Of the quick passage of our years!

To me it brings sad thoughts of one,
Who, in the summer's fading bloom,
Bright from the arms of love went down
To the dim silence of the tomb.

How often since has spring's soft shower
Revived the life in nature's breast,
And the sweet herb and tender flower
Have been renewed above her rest!

How many summer times have told
To mortal hearts their rapid flight,
Since first this heap of yellow mould
Shut out her beauty from my sight!

Since first, to love's sweet promise true,
My feet beside her pillow trod,
Till year by year the pathway grew
Deeper and deeper in the sod!

Now these neglected roses tell
Of no kind hand to tend them nigh;
Oh, God! I have not kept so well
My faith as in the years gone by.

But here to-day my step returns,
And, kneeling where these willows wave,
As the soft flame of sunrise burns
Down through the dim leaves to thy grave,

I cry, Forgive that I should prove
Forgetful of thy memory;
Forgive me, that a living love
Once came between my soul and thee!

For the weak heart that faintly yearned
For human love its life to cheer,
Baffled and bleeding has returned
To stifle down its crying here.

For, steadfast still, thy faith to me
Was one which earth could not estrange:
And, lost one! where the angels be,
I know affection may not change.

## STRENGTH OF SIN.

How lately and this beautiful earth
  Was shut by darkness from my sight,
And all the mighty arch of blue
  Was sparkling with its worlds of light.

Waning and waning, one by one
  They vanished as the day-star rose,
Till, lo! along the distant hills
  The fire of sunrise burns and glows.

And turning from the hosts of heaven
  To the calm beauty of the earth,
I feel what goodness must be His
  Who spoke its glories into birth.

More than our hearts can comprehend,
  Or our weak blinded eyes can see,
The wisdom and the love of God,
  How mighty and how vast they be!

Too fair for us to hate or leave
  This world His hand has placed us in,
But for the presence and the power
  Of that most fiery serpent, sin—

That first in Eden's peaceful shade
  Uncoiled its bright and deadly folds,
And living still, and unsubdued,
  Sends its dark poison through our souls.

But from his creatures, blind and lost,
  God never wholly turned aside,
As power to save us from the curse
  Was sent us when the Saviour died.

All that is left us under heaven,
  Hope of the lost and sin enslaved,
The only Name on earth that's given,
  Whereby the souls of men are saved.

Thanks unto God, that He was sent
  A sacred warfare to begin,
That in the end shall surely crush
  And bind the infernal strength of sin!

That by Him it shall be at last
  Out from this fair creation hurled,
Who gave its death-blow when the cross
  Was darkly planted in the world.

And thanks to Him, that when the soul
  In agony for mercy calls,
Right in the shadow of that cross
  The sunlight of His pardon falls.

## THE WOMEN AT THE SEPULCHRE.

Morn broke on Calvary, and the sun was flinging
 The earliest brightness from his locks abroad,
As the meek sisters came in sadness, bringing
 Gifts of sweet spices to anoint their Lord.

They who had loved his blessed precepts ever,
 And linger'd with him when the earth was gloom,
They were the faithful who reviled him never,
 "Last at the cross, and earliest at the tomb!"

I've sometimes thought I never could inherit
 A glorious mansion in the skies above:
For, oh! how weak and faltering is my spirit,
 Compared with such undying faith and love!

But, Father, cannot all that heavenly meekness,
 That deathless love which all things could endure,
Can it not plead before Thee, for the weakness
 Of one whose faith is oft so faint and poor?

## MELODY.

THE beautiful eve, in her sparkling tiara,
With dew-dropping fingers is closing the flower,
Where thou, oh! my white-bosomed bird of the prairie,
Art watching and waiting for me in our bower.

My heart, beating quick as the pulse of the ocean,
Outstrips e'en my courser, to see thee again;
Though his limbs are as lithe and as fleet in their motion
As the barb in the desert, or roe on the plain.

My heart feels no presage of evil or danger,
For thou never wouldst fly, lovely warbler, from me;
And I hid thee so well that the spoiler and stranger
Could track not the windings which lead me to thee.

Yet faster, my steed: for the starlight discloses
Our bower, but no minstrel its shadows among;—
Yes, something is fluttering like wings in the roses,
And, bird of my bosom! I hear thy sweet song.

## CHANGES.

UNDER the evening splendour
Of spring's sweet skies,
Learned I love's lesson tender—
From the maiden's eyes.

When the stars, like lovers meeting,
In the blue appeared,
And my heart, tumultuous beating,
Hoped and feared.

Then the passion, long dissembled,
My lip made known,
And the hand of the maiden trembled
In my own—

Till the tears that gushed unbidden,
Unrepressed,
And the crimson blush was hidden
On my breast.

And there in that vale elysian,
Through the summer bland,
We walked in a tranced vision,
Hand in hand.

There the evening shadows found us
Side by side,
While the glorious roses round us
Bloomed and died.

And when the bright sun, waning,
Dimly burned,—
When the wind with sad complaining,
In the valley mourned,—

When the bridal roses faded
In her hair,
And her brow was sweetly shaded
With a thought of care,—

Then with heart still fondly thrilling,
But with calmer bliss,
From the lip no more unwilling,
I claimed the kiss.

Then our dreams, with love o'erladen,
Were verified,
And dearer to me than the maiden
Grew the bride.

But when the dead leaves drifted
In that valley low,
And down from the cold sky sifted
The noiseless snow:

Where the hearts of the faithful moulder
With the dead,
They made her a pillow colder
Than the bridal bed.

And there at the spring's returning,
With the summer's glow,
When the autumn's sun is burning,
In the winter's snow,—

With the ghosts of the dim past ever
Gliding round,
Walk I in that vale as a river
That makes no sound.

---

## FEARS.

Hold me closer to thy bosom,
Let me feel thy clasping hand;
Wilder grows the night, and drearer—
Shall we never reach the land?

Thrice from dreams of broken slumber
Have I started in affright;
On the shore I never trembled
As I tremble here to-night.

Nay, 'tis not the haunting beauty
Of some lovely vision gone—
But the watches wear so heavy;
Leave me, leave me not alone!

Yes, I know the waves are calmer,
And the sky has lost its frown,
But the sharp reefs, ere the morning
We may strike them, and go down!

Said you that the dawn is breaking,
With its gray uncertain light?
Look! I dare not trust my vision—
Are the cliffs of home in sight?

Hush! I cannot, listening eager,
Hear the heavy billows roar;
We are standing in still water—
We are nearing to the shore!

Yes, above us, streaming seaward,
Shine the red lights of the tower;
We are anchored—we are mooring—
God be praised for such an hour!

## THE WATCHER.

'Tis the third summer that has gone,
Since first upon that sloping hill,
He listened for the feet of one
Whose coming he is waiting still.

All through the evenings warm and bland,
When the red sunset lights the skies,
Then first we see the watcher stand,
With hope reflected in his eyes:

Still waiting through the tranquil hours,
Till eve with fingers, fair and slight,
Has folded up to sleep the flowers,
And left them with the peaceful night.

But when the stars like fire-sparks glow
In the far pavement of the sky,
Then hope, that lingered on till now,
Fades slowly from his cheek and eye.

And when the still night, wearing on,
Has almost broken into day,
As if he knew she would not come,
He turns with mournful step away.

Oh, heavily, and dull, and slow,
  Such hours of anxious vigil wane:
God keep that watcher in his wo,
  Who looks for coming feet in vain.

'Twas on the morning of a day
  Sweet as the night-time ever nursed,
Her white arms filled with flowers of May,
  He saw the village maiden first.

Like the last hues of dying day,
  Which sunset from his path has rolled,
The roses of the summer lay
  Softly among her locks of gold.

Singing a soft and plaintive lay,
  She won him with her gentle tone,
And then he stole her heart away
  With voice as witching as her own.

And once, when the sweet stars as now
  Look calmly down upon that hill,
Their young hearts breathed the tender vow
  Which one has kept so faithful still.

And meeting nightly, 'twas not strange,
  But yet he dreamed not love could wane,
Or thought that human hearts might change,
  Until he waited there in vain.

And still, to meet her on that height,
  *He* lingers as in summers gone,
Till evening deepening into night,
  He wakes to find himself alone.

For none till now have ever told
  That watcher of expectant hours,
How long ago her locks of gold
  Were braided with the bridal flowers.

---

## CHALMERS.

In the hush of the desolate midnight,
  Leaving no brighter behind,
A noble light was stricken
  From the galaxy of mind.

As the red lights down in the water,
  When a boat shoots into the sea,
Or a star through the thin blue ether,
  He vanished silently.

Not the counsel of ghostly fathers
  Showed him the way he trod,
Not the picture of saints and martyrs,
  Nor the smile of the Mother of God;

Not the love-lighted brows of kindred,
  Nor the words of a faithful friend,
Opened up the way to his vision,
  And cheered him to the end.

As a God-fearing man, and holy,
  He had passed through the snares beneath,
And he needed no aid to strengthen
  His soul in the hour of death.

The steps of his faith were planted
  Where the waves in vain might beat,
While the waters of death rose darkly,
  And closed around his feet.

Not the "Save, or I perish!" of Peter,
  Was his as he faintly trod,
But the trust of that first blest martyr,
  Falling asleep in God.

And we may not mourn the brightness
  That is taken from our sky,
Which shall teach to the unborn ages
  The way to live and die.

## SONG.

THE first and loveliest star of even
  Shines on me with its first sweet light:
O thou, to whom my heart is given,
  What visions haunt thy soul to-night?

Dost thou, as this soft twilight steals
  So mildly over hill and plain,
Think of the hour we parted last,
  And wish me by thy side again?

I ask not that thy love should be
  As deep, as trusting as my own,
I do not ask that thou shouldst feel
  All that my woman's heart has known:

But if, for every thousand times
  My spirit fondly turns to thee,
One thought of thine to me is given,
  I doubt not thy fidelity.

For me, when on the hills alone,
  Or treading through the noisy mart,
There is no time, there is no place,
  But thou art with me in my heart.

I only think upon the past,
  Or dream of happier days to be,
And every hope and every fear
  Is something hoped or feared for thee.

# THE CONFESSION.

In the moonlight of the spring-time,
Trembling, blushing, half afraid,
Heard I first the fond confession
From the sweet lips of the maid.

As the roses of the summer,
By his warm embraces won,
Take a fairer, richer colour
From the glances of the sun;

So as, gazing, earnest, anxious,
I besought her but to speak,
Deep, and deeper burned the crimson
Of the blushes in her cheek;

Till at last, with happy impulse,
Impulse that she might not check,
As it softly thrilled and trembled,
Stole her white arm round my neck;

And with lips, that, half averted
From the lips that bent above,
Met the kiss of our betrothal,
Told the maiden of her love.

## THE ILLS OF LIFE.

How oft, when pursued by evils,
We falter and faint by the way,
But are fearless when, o'ertaken,
We pause, and turn at bay.

When storms in the distance have gathered,
I have trembled their wrath to meet,
Yet stood firm when the arrowy lightning
Has fallen at my feet.

My soul in the shadows of twilight
Has groaned beneath its load,
And felt at the solemn midnight
Secure in the hand of God.

I have been with friends who were cherished
All earthly things above,
Till I deemed the death-pangs lighter
Than the pangs of parting love.

Yet with one fearful struggle,
When at last the dread blow fell,
I have kept my heart from breaking,
And calmly said, Farewell!

I have looked at the grave, and shuddered
  For my kindred treading near,
And when their feet had entered,
  My soul forgot its fear.

Our ills are not so many
  Nor so hard to bear below,
But our suffering in dread of the future
  Is more than our present wo.

We see with our vision imperfect
  Such causes of doubt and fear—
Some yet that are far in the distance,
  And some that may never be near—

When, if we would trust in His wisdom
  Whose purpose we may not see,
We would find, whatever our trials,
  As our day our strength shall be.

## THE BRIDE.

LIKE the music of an arrow,
  Rushing, singing from the string,
Was the sound in the June roses
  Of each homeward cleaving wing.

Where the leaves were softly parted
  By a hand of snowy grace,
Letting in a shower of sunlight
  Brightly o'er an eager face;

O'er the young face of a maiden,
  Touched by changing hope and fear,
As the sound of rapid hoof-strokes,
  Nearing, fell upon the ear.

White robes softly heaving, fluttering,
  O'er her bosom's rise of snow,
Spoke the strange and soft confession
  Of the beating heart below.

And the face had sweet revealings,
  Sweeter than the lip may speak,
For the soft fires of confession
  Lit their crimson in the cheek.

Not for friend, and not for brother,
  Kept she eager vigil there;
Not for friend, and not for brother,
  Gleamed the roses in her hair.

* * * * *

Myriad frost-sparks fire-like glittered
  In the keen and bitter air,
And no wild-bird, dropping downward,
  Stirred the branches cold and bare.

Flaming in the glorious forehead
  Of the midnight, high and lone,
Starry constellations, steadfast,
  Yet like burning jewels shone;

When, from a sick couch uplifted,
  A thin hand, most snowy white,
Parted back the curtains softly,
  Letting in the pallid light.

Eyes of more than mortal brightness
  Spoke the waiting heart's desire,
And the hollow cheeks were lighted
  With a quick, consuming fire.

That young watcher in the roses,
  Of the earnest eye and brow,
Keeps again her anxious vigil;
  Who shall end its moments now?

Lo! the breast is softly trembling,
But with hope that has no fear:
By that happy smile the Presence
She hath waited for is near!

For a bridegroom hath she tarried;
Bring the roses for her brow;
Though no human passion answers
To his icy kisses now.

Bride of earth! here, hoping, fearing,
Evil were thy days, and vain;
Bride of heaven! for blest fruition
Thou shalt never wait again.

## REMEMBRANCE.

I HAVE struggled long with weakness,
But my heart is free at last;
Never more will it be haunted
With the phantoms of the past.

Never more, from fairest maiden,
The light witchery of a word
Shall thrill my heart with rapture,
When its magic tones are heard.

And that heart, so long made heavy
With inquietude and wo,
From its fetters loosed, is ringing,
Like a quick shaft from the bow.

Forgotten be the trusted
That have lightly broke their trust;
And the dreams that I have cherished,
Let them perish in the dust!

Yet there was one fair maiden,
Sweetest vision of my youth,
She was lovely when I loved her,
And her words were like the truth.

And they may have torn her from me;
  She was faithful once, I know—
No, she smiled beside the altar,
  And 'twas not to hide her wo!

And how can she, smiling, meet me
  With that fearless, open brow?
'Twas like heaven, of old, to kiss it,
  'Twould be heaven to kiss it now.

Pause, remembrance, since for ever,
  Leila, dreams of thee are sin—
Oh, I thought my heart was stronger
  Till I paused and looked within!

THE END.

www.ingramcontent.com/pod-product-compliance
Lightning Source LLC
LaVergne TN
LVHW010247110826
845151LV00004B/1412

* 9 7 8 1 4 2 5 5 2 3 3 1 2 *